Teaching History with Message Movies

Teaching History with . . . Series

Series Editor: Cynthia J. Miller

Teaching History with Musicals, by Kathryn Edney, 2017.
Teaching History with Newsreels and Public Service Shorts, by Aaron Gulyas, 2017.
Teaching History with Science Fiction Films, by A. Bowdoin Van Riper, 2017.
Teaching History with Message Movies, by Jennifer Frost and Steven Alan Carr, 2018.

Teaching History with Message Movies

Jennifer Frost
Steven Alan Carr

ROWMAN & LITTLEFIELD
Lanham • Boulder • New York • London

Published by Rowman & Littlefield
An imprint of The Rowman & Littlefield Publishing Group, Inc.
4501 Forbes Boulevard, Suite 200, Lanham, Maryland 20706
www.rowman.com

Unit A, Whitacre Mews, 26-34 Stannary Street, London SE11 4AB

Copyright © 2018 by Jennifer Frost and Steven Alan Carr

All rights reserved. No part of this book may be reproduced in any form or by any electronic or mechanical means, including information storage and retrieval systems, without written permission from the publisher, except by a reviewer who may quote passages in a review.

British Library Cataloguing in Publication Information Available

Library of Congress Cataloging-in-Publication Data Available

ISBN 978-1-4422-7838-7 (pbk. : alk. paper) | ISBN 978-1-4422-7839-4 (ebook)

∞ ™ The paper used in this publication meets the minimum requirements of American National Standard for Information Sciences Permanence of Paper for Printed Library Materials, ANSI/NISO Z39.48-1992.

Printed in the United States of America

Contents

Acknowledgments	vii
Introduction	ix
CONCEPTS	1
1 A Brief History of the Message Movie, or Social Problem Film, in Hollywood	3
2 Concepts and Conventions of the Social Problem Film	15
TOPICS OVER TIME	23
3 Labor and Class Conflict, according to Hollywood	25
4 Women, Sex, and Family Conflict on Film	41
5 Projecting Racial and Ethnic Prejudice in the Social Problem Film	57
6 Screening Private Illness and Public Health	69
7 Crime at the Movies	83
DOCUMENTS	95
Social Problem Film Paper Sample Worksheet	97
Sample Syllabus: Teaching History through Message Movies	99
Message Movies for Classroom Use	105
Index	113
About the Authors	117

Acknowledgments

Our biggest thanks go to our editor, Cynthia Miller, who inspired the project in the first place and then has been unfailingly patient and encouraging as we brought the book to completion. We both appreciate having had this opportunity to work together on a book that brings together our fascination with the "message movie" or social problem film and our love of teaching film and history to our students. Our wonderfully sustaining collaboration began with a chance conversation at a Society for Cinema and Media Studies meeting and has yielded many new insights and rewards.

Thank you to my students Liam Appleton, Katie Cammell, and Hui Yu, who conducted exemplary primary and secondary research for the book, and to the Faculty of Arts at the University of Auckland for funding their research assistance. I also appreciate my family, Paul, Cealagh, and Luc Taillon, who spurred me on in the process of writing. —JF

Thanks to my colleagues and students in the Department of Communication at Purdue University Fort Wayne for listening to my harebrained schemes and crackpot ideas. Thanks to my family and extended families: my parents, Bill and Maxine; my brothers, Jonathan and Daniel, and their respective families; and last, but not least, Nancy, who somehow manages to put up with me after nearly a quarter of a century. —SC

Introduction

"If you want to send a message, call Western Union," or so goes an old Hollywood adage. Movies provide amusing cultural entertainment, according to the American film industry, rather than enlightened social awareness. But of course movies do more than entertain, and they all carry messages. Over more than a century, many Hollywood filmmakers explicitly set out to make "message movies," in which a social statement is as important as the characters or the plot. One type of message movie is the so-called social problem film, a genre of films that take as their subject a problem or conflict in society, such as racism or alcoholism. By illuminating contemporary social issues and conditions, these films make excellent primary sources or cultural artifacts for the study of US history in the 20th and 21st centuries.

This book is designed to provide teachers and students with the opportunity to examine Hollywood social problem films as historians, within the larger context of US social and cultural history. Organized chronologically and thematically, it situates the production and consumption of significant Hollywood social problem films within their specific historical contexts and analyzes these films for what they can reveal about the conditions that produced them, attracted audiences to them, and shaped their reception. With the assumption that Hollywood films both reflected and affected American society and history, but in "highly mediated and extremely complex" ways, as John Belton has argued,[1] we will ask of each film, What can this source tell us about the people, society, and culture that created it?

Although all movies tell us something, social problem films provide useful insights into what Americans considered the most pressing concerns of their day and why they thought so. This book will interrogate change and continuity over time in the definitions of America's social problems, according to Hollywood. Some of these social problems were considered new in their time and place. Others continued older conflicts. All were created by or connected to ongoing social change, for example industrialization or urbanization. Yet not every social issue or development came to be defined as a "problem" or to be defined as such by every American. In this process, the US film industry and individual filmmakers played an influential role by highlighting and even heightening certain concerns in their films.

But they did not operate alone; the commentaries and responses of film reviewers and filmgoers also contributed to this process. Hollywood movies intersect with the larger public sphere and illuminate the play of ideas and interests in US history. The public discussions and debates around these films circulated and contested their definitions of social problems.[2] Published film reviews and news reports provide evidence of how these films were received by critics and journalists. With regard to the popular audience, the challenges of uncovering "real cinema spectators" from the past are well known in historical film studies.[3] Yet audience response does appear in the press coverage of movies and can illuminate a broader range of reception possibilities at the time.

Also of interest are the analyses of causes and the proposed solutions to social problems found in Hollywood movies and how these are shaped by their historical context. Even as message movies are dramatic fictional films designed to sell tickets to a moviegoing audience, they present reasons why a problem has arisen and what can be done to resolve it. For many scholars of the social problem film, including Peter Roffman, Jim Purdy, and Steve Neale, Hollywood's analysis of social problems has been "glib." And instead of pragmatic solutions to real social problems, these films offer "the actual resolution of personal ones."[4] Or the solution is completely unrealistic, as when a rich benefactor swoops in to save the day. Even so, the causes and solutions offered in social problem films illuminate popular—and even at times academic—understandings of social reality and the spectrum of possibilities for resolution at that historical moment.

Political ideology further shapes filmmakers' approaches and audience response to social problems in movies. The genre has been closely linked to social reform movements and eras in US history. The films originated in the era of Progressive reform during the first two decades of the 20th century, as Kevin Brownlow and Kay Sloan found among silent films.[5] They flourished during the populist "talkies" of the 1930s Great Depression period, the focus of Roffman and Purdy's study. From the 1940s on, the genre was associated with liberalism. As liberalism waxed and waned over the middle decades of the 20th century, the films often mirrored these developments. Chris Cagle's recent book surveys this time period.[6] The genre's resurgence later in the century and especially in the 21st century connected to new social movements such as feminism and environmentalism. Today many of the most exciting social problem films take on global concerns, reflecting that today's challenges require a broad, international perspective.

Exploring these ideological connections will help to explain the prescriptive elements of social problem films. One of the central defining features of these films is their didacticism: they aim to teach viewers a lesson.[7] Filmmakers directly address and seek to persuade their audiences. They want filmgoers to come away from the theater with a clear lesson learned about how to prevent or correct failings in public life, social institutions, or personal behavior. These lessons reveal what filmmakers believed *ought* to be the character and conditions of American society. But critical and popular audiences did not always respond favorably to these prescriptions for change. Whether they accepted, rejected, or amended the prescription further illuminates the film's ideological content and historical context.

Even as social problem films are prescriptive, they are also often richly descriptive of what actually existed in that time and place. This feature is due to the genre's tendency toward realism both in subject matter and style.[8] To convince filmgoers of the urgency of a contemporary social problem, it must be presented as existing in the real world with real consequences for real people. This obligation shaped plot and character development, as well as mise-en-scène (all that appears in or frames the cinematic space). Although the realism of story lines and characters could be compromised by the requirements of drama, the settings, props, and costumes in social problem films often accurately captured the "look and feel" of the period depicted.[9] This depiction of physical reality and material conditions—say, a rundown urban tenement or a gleaming mental hospital—provides "precious historical evidence," Brownlow noted.[10]

Watching these films can immerse us in the past, especially if we identify or empathize with the characters. Like all movies, social problem films seek to draw spectators into the plot through sympathetic characters. Guarding against overidentification or viewing characters through the lens of the present, we can gain an intimate sense of what it may have been like to experience these social problems. By fostering historical empathy, even with fictional characters and melodramatic plots, these films can lead to greater awareness of the range of contemporary perspectives or points of view. Such awareness allows for a deeper understanding of the choices available to historical actors and the consequences of their actions. Using film to forge an emotional connection to the past for students also can expand intellectual comprehension of history.

Studying American social problem films, then, teaches both historical content and skills. Each of the five core chapters in this book cover topics over time: labor and class conflict; women, sex, and family conflict; racial and ethnic prejudice; physical and mental illness; and crime. These chapters integrate how to teach specific films, within their historical contexts and using key historical and film literacy skills. These chapters are preceded with two chapters dedicated to understanding the genre of the social problem film, with a brief historical overview, as well as a discussion of key themes and concepts. The book ends with useful materials for the classroom.

A variety of teaching ideas are included in the chapters in part 2, "Topics over Time," due to the fact that we bring different scholarly backgrounds to this project. Jennifer is a US historian who teaches film, whereas Steve is a radio-film-television scholar who engages with history. Our scholarly backgrounds mean we offer different readings of film and different approaches to teaching. Jennifer's primary interest in historical context and reception means she draws heavily on primary historical sources to situate and teach the films in chapters 4 and 6. Steve offers textual readings of the films and an emphasis on production factors in chapters 3, 5, and 7, modeling how to develop an analysis and argument about social problem film. This variety offers readers the opportunity to see two different methodological and pedagogical approaches at work. Readers can dip into the separate chapters or read the book from start to finish. All of the teaching ideas presented can be used with any film of your choice, so much can be gained from the latter strategy!

In selecting films for inclusion in *Teaching History with Message Movies*, we have decided to focus on US films, and specifically Hollywood feature films, not documentaries. Although the impulse and purpose behind social problem films are related to those of documentary films—"to inform and educate citizens, by exploring contemporary concerns through the medium of film"[11]—our focus is on fiction films. Like early scholars, we also are concerned with social issues and conditions contemporary to the period in which actual audiences would have seen those films, but we did include selected historical films—that is, films based on actual historical personages and events. Finally, political films—where an individual interacts with government or a political movement—also can be categorized as "message movies." We have chosen to exclude this category, however. Although politics and government remain relevant to our study, our focus emphasizes the important role these films play in addressing broader social institutions and identities related to class, race and ethnicity, gender and the family, illness, and crime.

NOTES

1. John Belton, *American Cinema/American Culture* (New York: McGraw-Hill, 1994), xxi.
2. Jason Mittell, "A Cultural Approach to Television Genre Theory," *Cinema Journal* 40 (Spring 2001): 9.
3. Jackie Stacey, *Star Gazing: Hollywood Cinema and Female Spectatorship* (London and New York: Routledge, 1994), 49–79.

4. Peter Roffman and Jim Purdy, *The Hollywood Social Problem Film: Madness, Despair and Politics from the Depression to the Fifties* (Bloomington: Indiana University Press, 1981), viii; Steve Neale, *Genre and Hollywood* (London and New York: Routledge, 2000), 108.

5. Kevin Brownlow, *Behind the Mask of Innocence* (New York: Knopf, 1990); Kay Sloan, *The Loud Silents: Origins of the Social Problem Film* (Urbana: University of Illinois Press, 1998).

6. Chris Cagle, *Sociology on Film: Postwar Hollywood's Prestige Commodity* (New Brunswick, NJ: Rutgers University Press, 2017).

7. Roffman and Purdy, *Hollywood Social Problem Film*, viii.

8. Ibid., 11.

9. Robert A. Rosenstone, *Visions of the Past: The Challenge of Film to Our Idea of History* (Cambridge, MA: Harvard University Press, 1995), 59–60.

10. Brownlow, *Behind the Mask of Innocence*, xxi.

11. Samantha Lay, *British Social Realism: From Documentary to Brit-Grit* (London: Wallflower Press, 2002), 55.

WORKS CITED

Belton, John. *American Cinema/American Culture*. New York: McGraw-Hill, 1994.

Brownlow, Kevin. *Behind the Mask of Innocence*. New York: Knopf, 1990.

Cagle, Chris. *Sociology on Film: Postwar Hollywood's Prestige Commodity*. New Brunswick, NJ: Rutgers University Press, 2017.

Lay, Samantha. *British Social Realism: From Documentary to Brit-Grit*. London: Wallflower Press, 2002.

Mittell, Jason. "A Cultural Approach to Television Genre Theory." *Cinema Journal* 40 (Spring 2001): 3–24.

Neale, Steve. *Genre and Hollywood*. London and New York: Routledge, 2000.

Roffman, Peter, and Jim Purdy. *The Hollywood Social Problem Film: Madness, Despair and Politics from the Depression to the Fifties*. Bloomington: Indiana University Press, 1981.

Rosenstone, Robert A. *Visions of the Past: The Challenge of Film to Our Idea of History*. Cambridge, MA: Harvard University Press, 1995.

Sloan, Kay. *The Loud Silents: Origins of the Social Problem Film*. Urbana: University of Illinois Press, 1998.

Stacey, Jackie. *Star Gazing: Hollywood Cinema and Female Spectatorship*. London and New York: Routledge, 1994.

CONCEPTS

Chapter One

A Brief History of the Message Movie, or Social Problem Film, in Hollywood

The genre of the social problem film has a long history in the US motion picture industry, even before the industry moved to Hollywood, California. They were not always called "social problem" films. Within the early motion picture industry, as film historian Kevin Brownlow notes, they were known as "sociological" or "thought" films, and he uses the term *social film*.[1] The social problem film is a capacious genre, known for "an extensive crossing of genres" and even as a "hybrid" genre. Therefore, a variety of films can fall within the category, ranging from comedies to crime films.[2] What allows these films to be grouped and described as social problem films is their subject matter: the story of an individual or groups confronting a social problem or conflict. While our next chapter lays out the themes and conventions that help to define the genre—and addresses the scholarly debate about whether it is, in fact, a "genre"—this chapter provides a brief history of the US social problem film in the 20th and 21st centuries.

In surveying this history, the most prominent historical developments that emerges in connection with the social problem film are movements for social reform. Although reform efforts have existed throughout US history, there are eras dominated by widespread calls for—and organizing to achieve— reform in response to social change. It is during these eras over the past century that the social problem film has flourished: producers are interested in making these films, and audiences are keen to see them. "If social change is impossible, then problem films are irrelevant," argue Peter Roffman and Jim Purdy.[3] In those historical moments when reform and change seemed most possible, these films found an audience and influenced public discussion of the problems they addressed. These key periods include the Progressive Era at the start of the 20th century, the Great Depression and New Deal of the 1930s, the World War II and Cold War period, the 1960s and 1970s, and the turn of the 21st century.

Social problem films were made and received within these specific historical contexts but also within distinct industrial circumstances. Conditions in the American film industry—which in the 1910s came to be located in Southern California and was soon to be called "Hollywood"—further shaped the genre. Our historical examination traces changes in technology; in the organization of production, distribution, and exhibition; and in public opinion and government regulation, including censorship. A truism of film studies is that both historical and industrial developments must be considered to understand Hollywood's filmmaking practice and output, including with regard to genre. Steve Neale argues that "genre is a multi-dimensional phenomenon."[4] Here and in subsequent chapters, we will show how a complex interplay of factors influence and are revealed in the production and reception of American social problem films over time.

PROGRESSIVE ERA, 1900–1920

The films that later come to be called "social problem" films reflect and, in turn, provide insights into the US reform mood and movements of the early 20th century. This idea and impulse toward reform was called "Progressivism." It was a response to the emergence of modern America and involved "the search for order," as historian Robert Wiebe has defined it, in the face of major changes in the economy, politics, society, and culture.[5] To achieve order, Progressive activists and policymakers advanced a new concept of government. Instead of a small, "laissez faire" government with limited powers, they advocated a larger government capable of intervening and regulating the economy and society. Although the era had its advocates for radical and revolutionary politics, the Progressive search for order occurred within the existing political and economic systems of representative democracy and industrial capitalism. Progressivism also was not one movement but rather a diverse set of reform efforts. Suffrage for women and labor laws guaranteeing minimum wages, maximum hours, and outlawing child labor coexisted with anti-immigration measures and laws disenfranchising and segregating African Americans. This mix of progress and reaction reveals the so-called paradox of Progressivism.[6]

The early US film industry evolved within this historical context. Thanks to innovators like Thomas Edison, motion pictures got started in the 1890s with the kinetoscope, a device that allowed an individual to watch very short films—lasting only 35–40 seconds—through a peephole. But soon movies began to be projected on screens, a development in 1896 that the *New York Times* considered "wonderfully real and singularly exhilarating."[7] These early films presented simple scenes and spectacles, like a comic boxing match or waves breaking on a beach, in what film historian Tom Gunning calls "the cinema of attractions."[8] As film technology developed, motion pictures lengthened. At the same time, the language of film emerged—created by filmmakers and learned by filmgoers. Soon more complex storytelling became possible, and narrative came to characterize American film during the first decade of the 20th century. Film production involved many entities—large and small movie companies, political organizations, social groups, and prominent individuals—and initially centered in New York, the nation's theatrical capital. This connection to Broadway and vaudeville theater had a profound effect on style and storytelling in early American film, even as movies were silent—that is, lacking in synchronized sound. This effect included several transfers from stage to screen, including personnel, specific story content, and genres.

Famous theatrical genres, like melodrama and comedy, transferred to early film and, together with "topical" theater or drama, were sources for the social problem film genre. "The earliest audiences," scholar Kay Sloan argues, "pushed their coins across box office windows to watch melodramas and comedies that often celebrated characters who literally animated the social and political dilemmas of the Progressive Era."[9] Right from the start, the social problem film genre demonstrated flexibility by overlapping with other genres. It also had topical immediacy, with story lines about poverty, child labor, drug and alcohol addiction, and prostitution drawn from newspaper headlines. By taking on contemporary concerns, these films shared a purpose with investigative journalists who exposed corruption and injustice in American society and were called "muckrakers" by President Theodore Roosevelt. Indeed, journalists often directly contributed to "muckraking cinema." Upton Sinclair, who revealed the horrific working and sanitary conditions in the meatpacking industry in *The Jungle*, adapted his 1906 novel and its radical politics into a 1913 film. Silent social problem films also generally presented clear, linear narratives, with dramatic conflicts brought to a tidy resolution. In *Capital Versus Labor* (1910), for example, a minister brokers peace between greedy employers and ill-treated employees.

The contemporary relevance of these films provoked public discussion and debate and prompted early efforts to regulate and censor the motion picture industry. Commentators variously responded to a film's subject, meaning, and impact. A reviewer of *In the Grip of Alcohol* (1912) strongly disliked "gruesome, heartbreaking tragedies" but admitted such films "may perhaps be a terrific force for good."[10] The reception of what historian Steven J. Ross calls "labor-capital films" depended upon the producers' pro- or anti-union stances.[11] For some Progressive reformers, filmmakers, and contemporaries, motion pictures could contribute to moral and social uplift. But for others, the movies were a menace to morality and social order, especially given the size of their audience. In 1910, an estimated 26 million Americans—about one-fifth of the total population—visited a "nickelodeon" every week. Public opinion about the power of motion pictures led to censorship on the local level beginning in 1907. Fierce debate about whether film censorship violated the First Amendment to the US Constitution culminated in a Supreme Court decision in *Mutual Film Corporation v. Ohio Industrial Commission* (1915). The court ruled that motion pictures were not covered by constitutional protections of freedom of speech and press. Instead, the "exhibition of motion pictures is a business, plain and simple, originated and conducted for profit."[12] Early movie censorship exemplified the paradoxical nature of Progressive reform.

THE GREAT DEPRESSION AND THE NEW DEAL, 1930s

Social problem films decreased along with Progressive reform in the 1920s but increased again during the following decade of economic crisis and reform. Notable films made in the 1920s still took on relevant social issues, however. Just as political pressure grew for legislation restricting immigration, *Hungry Hearts* (1922) told a sympathetic story of a Jewish immigrant family adapting to their new life in New York, with all the hardships and heartbreak that entailed. Yet scholars agree such films were no longer as popular or numerous as they previously had been or as they would soon be again. Partly this was due the motion picture industry's consolidation into eight major companies in the 1920s, with film production in Hollywood and financial decision-making in New York. These big companies achieved near-monopolistic control of the industry, extending from production through distribution to exhibition. They established the "star system," whereby stars sold the movies and the industry sold the stars.[13] By the end of the decade, an estimated 90 million Americans attended the movies every week. Then hard times hit, with the stock market crash of 1929 signaling deep fault lines in the US economy.

The Great Depression's unprecedented economic problems and despair spurred the New Deal, a set of reforms designed to solve those problems. The unemployment rate rose from 3.2% in 1929 to 23.6% in 1932. As unemployment grew, so did homelessness and starvation. Such economic devastation had a profound emotional and psychological impact on American individuals, families, and society as a whole. Widespread fear existed that the Depression had destroyed family relations and men's economic role as family breadwinners. It even called into question what was the American Dream—that if you work hard and live an upstanding, moral life, you'll succeed, achieving a decent standard of living. The New Deal aimed to restore the American Dream. Heralded by Franklin Delano Roosevelt, elected president in 1932 and reelected three more times, the New Deal realized the Progressive concept of government. The US federal government assumed major responsibilities for regulating the economy and ensuring the welfare of its citizens. Roosevelt and other New Deal advocates justified these changes as supporting hardworking common people, or as FDR put it, "the forgotten man."

Such populist politics affected and reflected a variety of American films of the 1930s, a period often called Hollywood's "golden age." With the advent of synchronized sound technology in the late 1920s, the industry entered a new phase of innovation and creativity. Now filmmakers could explore their subjects in more detail, using snappy spoken dialogue instead of simply written titles. The "talkies," as early sound films were called, became the nation's most popular form of entertainment.[14] But the Great Depression had a major impact on film industry. The expense of transitioning to sound movies and of building and purchasing theaters to control exhibition had placed financial demands on the big studios. When ticket sales dropped to an average of 60 million per week, Hollywood experienced its own hard times. Studios began to lose money and cut costs, including firing personnel. They worked harder to get spectators into theaters with movies connected to contemporary experiences and settings. Social problem films again took hold with cycles of gangster films and so-called fallen woman films in the early 1930s. Crime and sex sold tickets and exposed the underside of American life. Films about poverty and labor conflict, such as *The Grapes of Wrath* (1940), adapted from the prize-winning John Steinbeck novel, highlighted the social inequalities impelling New Deal reforms.

The "cultural force that the problem film represented" during this era cannot be underestimated, Roffman and Purdy argue.[15] As during the Progressive Era, these films led to conversation and controversy. Moral reformers and religious groups responded to the early cycles of social problem films with calls for stricter enforcement of the industry's system of censorship. Beginning with the Supreme Court's *Mutual* decision in 1915, the motion picture industry opted for self-regulation rather than government censorship. Using first New York's National Board of Review and then Will Hays, the head of the Motion Picture Producers and Distributors of America, Hollywood aimed to "clean up the movies." "The Don'ts and Be Carefuls" circulated for producers in the 1920s.[16] Under pressure, especially from the Roman Catholic Legion of Decency, the list evolved into the Production Code of 1930, with enforcement finally coming with the Production Code Administration (PCA) in 1934. For 20 years, a devout Catholic, Joseph Breen, ran the PCA office. Negotiation with the "Breen office" became part of the Hollywood production process. This process, in turn, shaped the populist plots and political ideology of the social problem films of the late 1930s and early 1940s.

FROM WORLD WAR TO COLD WAR, 1940–1960

Hollywood still portrayed American domestic social problems at the start of the 1940s, but US entry into World War II changed that. From 1942 to 1945, Roffman and Purdy contend, "the social problem film all but disappeared and was absorbed into the wartime propaganda films."[17] Such propaganda contributed to World War II being remembered as "the good war." Although it is difficult to consider any war "good"—much less a war that led to some 50 million military and civilian deaths worldwide—the United States vitally contributed to the defense of democracy against the attacks of fascist Germany, Italy, and Japan and fully succeeded. By projecting the idea of the good war to Americans and their allies, Hollywood movies showed the United States as a democratic country and a force for good in the world. This portrayal affected moviemaking after the war's end, with the social problem film genre enjoying a brief renaissance. These filmmakers sought to make real the wartime rhetoric of liberal democracy and confronted racial and ethnic inequality, as well as social intolerance of individual problems, such as war trauma, alcoholism, and mental illness. The genre's resurgence mostly ended with the heating up of the Cold War. The output of social problem films fell during the 1950s due to anti-Communists targeting such films as "Communist propaganda."

For Hollywood, the 1940s was a period of "boom and bust," as Thomas Schatz puts it, and the bust continued throughout the 1950s.[18] During World War II, the motion picture industry had boomed. The movies were one of the few places where Americans could spend their wartime income, and Hollywood achieved a peak in popularity and profits. It did not last, however, and the descent was steep. A series of postwar shocks jolted the industry. Box office receipts declined as filmgoers moved to the suburbs, bought televisions, and stayed home. At the same time, an antitrust case against the big movie companies and their control of production, distribution, and exhibition resulted in the *United States v. Paramount Pictures, Inc.* decision in 1948; it forced those companies who owned theater chains to divest, thus losing a crucial source of income. Finally, the House Un-American Activities Committee (HUAC) held its first postwar hearings to investigate Communism and subversion in the motion picture industry in October 1947. These hearings featured the Hollywood Ten, ten so-called unfriendly witnesses who refused to testify. One outcome was the establishment of the Hollywood blacklist to ensure that no persons espousing or supporting Left and often even liberal political ideas were employed in the motion picture industry.

The Hollywood Ten were all members or former members of the US Communist Party and had been involved in making motion pictures aimed at contributing to social change and reform. "They wanted to improve the plight of poor and working people, especially minorities, and to end racism and discrimination," argues scholar Stephen Vaughn.[19] Screenwriter John Howard Lawson's *Sahara* (1943) and Albert Maltz's screenplay for *The House I Live In* (1945) offered more positive representations of racial and ethnic minorities, for example. Producer Adrian Scott and director Edward Dmytryk made *Crossfire*, a 1947 film that powerfully criticized American racism and anti-Semitism. An important film that earned five Oscar nominations, *Crossfire* was edged out for Best Picture that year by another social problem film about anti-Semitism, *Gentleman's Agreement*. Despite the leftist political commitments of the Hollywood Ten, the ideological content of these films was decidedly liberal. This liberalism was mainly due to the collaborative nature of the production process in Hollywood, including the PCA's involvement. That fact did not prevent anti-Communists from seeing "Red propaganda" in these and other postwar social problem films and campaigning against them.

Out of this volatile mix of industry and political developments came opportunities for independent producers to engage with the genre. With the old Hollywood studios under increasing pressure, a new postwar generation of independent producers took advantage of the business and creative openings in the industry. The "independents," as they were called, needed to keep costs low, and they could not afford to compete with the major studios on big-budget musicals or westerns. Instead, they set out to make their mark with less expensive social problem films. Even when under attack from anti-Communists, liberal producers like Stanley Kramer sought to engage audiences with dramatic narratives about contemporary topics in a realist style. The genre had long tended toward realism in subject and style, but the prevalence of newsreels and other documentaries during World War II reinforced this tendency. Reviewers and commentators often complimented such realism, as scholar Chris Cagle finds. *Newsweek* magazine praised Billy Wilder's movie about alcoholism, *The Lost Weekend* (1945), for "realistic sets." The "street scenes, which were photographed in New York, are the real thing." Cagle also points out that social problem films were "Hollywood's prestige commodity" during this period.[20] But not for long.

THE SIXTIES AND THE SEVENTIES, 1960–1980

During the 1960s and 1970s, young Americans born during the baby boom after World War II brought a new agenda and aesthetic to the nation and to Hollywood. They often were persuaded by the messages of the prestigious liberal social problem films of their youth in the 1950s. But as they later came of age, they began to feel dissuaded from the genre and its politics. The 1960s and the 1970s can be considered as a time period or a series of developments in domestic and foreign policy, such as civil rights legislation and the Vietnam War. Yet the era is best understood as a mood or a spirit, for social and cultural change and for personal and political transformation. Due to their sheer numbers, the baby boom generation significantly shaped American culture and politics. To a certain degree, a generation gap developed between young people and their values and goals and that of their parents. Although far from a universal experience, many came to question and criticize the American Dream as empty materialism or conformist living. To them, political liberalism was complicit in US racism and imperialism. Instead, they sought to explore and experience life in new ways through New Left politics and the "hippie" counterculture.

It is often observed that television—by 1960, the nation's primary entertainment medium—captured the 1960s and 1970s the best, but mainstream and independent Hollywood films depicted cultural and political developments in these decades too. In fact, they had to. By 1960, average weekly attendance at the movies had dropped to 40 million, less than half of what it had been at the end of World War II. By 1970, attendance had fallen again, to only 20 million per week. The number of films made also declined, bottoming out with 143 in 1963. Major studios went out of business or were purchased by big corporate conglomerates. Yet the industry launched a surprising revival in the 1970s. A new generation of filmmakers brought new stories, subjects, and filmmaking techniques to the movie capital. They also had more freedom to explore, with the end of the Production Code and the PCA's oversight and its replacement with a ratings system, as used today. In New Hollywood, the blockbuster—a big-budget film that attracts large audiences at home and abroad, like Steven Spielberg's *Jaws* (1975)—coexisted with "smaller, more idiosyncratic films" by directors like Robert Altman and Martin Scorsese.[21]

Social problem films continued to be produced during this period, but they were far fewer in number. Their reception was also hotly contested, largely owing to the waning of liberalism over the 1960s. Stanley Kramer's 1967 film, *Guess Who's Coming to Dinner*, exemplified the new cultural and political terrain. The film tells the story of a liberal, middle-aged white couple in San Francisco coming to terms with their daughter's marriage to an African American man. Kramer and his filmmaking colleagues considered this message to be very current in 1967. In fact, only six months earlier, the US Supreme Court had struck down as unconstitutional laws prohibiting interracial marriage in *Loving v. Virginia* (1967); this right to marry was considered a civil rights victory. Yet for many critics and commentators, the film's message was long outdated and only superficially addressed racial problems in the United States. As political events and developments increasingly discredited American liberalism as having the answers to social problems—and some Americans even blamed liberalism for the nation's problems—the ideological content of the genre diversified.

Together with the opening up of the film industry—at least for a while—more politically radical, black, and feminist independent films began to be made. At the same time, conservative social problem films about crime, such as the Dirty Harry films (1972–1977), starring Clint Eastwood, and Michael Winner's *Death Wish* (1974), found success with a mainstream audience. As Michael Ryan and Douglas Kellner persuasively argue, these films tended to find the causes of crime in "evil human nature" with retaliatory, even redemptive violence the only answer. Such conservative crime films further indicted the "more humane ways of dealing with crime" favored by liberals.[22] Films about American veterans of the Vietnam War returning to the United States and readjusting—or not—to family and social life also appeared in the 1970s. These films reflected the political divide between liberalism and conservatism, as demonstrated by two movies released in 1978. *Coming Home*, a quintessentially liberal film, advanced antiwar and feminist perspectives, while *Deer Hunter*'s interpretation of the war mirrored conservative arguments. All of these films took advantage of Hollywood's new ratings system to portray sex and violence more explicitly than formerly allowed. The politics and explicitness of 1970s social problem films prompted much public debate about what contemporary issues and concerns were tackled and how they were depicted.

THE TURN OF THE 21ST CENTURY

The ideological diversity evident in Hollywood's social problem films in the 1970s corresponded to that of the larger American society and continued into the next era. The 1980s were dominated by the political ascendance of the conservative wing of the Republican Party, symbolized by President Ronald Reagan. A former Hollywood actor, Reagan occupied the Oval Office for most of the decade. But the very next decade years, the 1990s, have been called "the Clinton Years," named after President Bill Clinton, who also served two terms in office. A self-styled "New Democrat," Clinton distanced himself from the liberalism of the 1960s and moved his political party to the center. He shared policy priorities with his Republican rivals, such as rolling back social welfare, increasing criminal punishments, and fostering economic globalization. The 21st century saw a Republican return to the presidency in 2000, followed by a Democrat in 2008, and then another Republican in 2016. This political division and back-and-forth coexisted with a multiplicity of identity and activist groups, who empowered and expressed themselves on a range of contemporary concerns. For good reasons, historian Daniel T. Rogers calls this era of political turmoil and culture wars "the Age of Fracture."[23]

For Hollywood, this fracturing of American society may have shattered the notion of a cohesive national audience for the movies, but the big corporate conglomerates that dominated the motion picture industry were able to grow their global audience. International sales became more important than the domestic market and contributed to the reign of big, action-packed blockbusters, popular both at home and abroad. The major companies also maintained their control over national and international distribution networks. "Distribution," according to scholar Geoff King, "has become the key strategic source of control over the industry."[24] Revenue from distribution underwrote the fundamental role the big Hollywood companies play in film financing. Even so, opportunities opened up for creative niche productions. New technologies contributed. Video and then digital cameras made it easier and less expensive to make a movie, and audiences now had a choice of viewing experiences. They could watch a movie in a theater or at home through a videocassette player, then through a digital video disc (DVD) player, and later by streaming through the internet. Capitalizing on these new technologies, independent filmmakers built a full-fledged "indie movement." Steven Soderbergh's pathbreaking *Sex, Lies, and Videotape* (1989) pointed the way.

Soderbergh's film debuted at the Sundance Festival, which exhibits and encourages innovative filmmaking that may "even lead to social change."[25] With new participants and institutions, the indie movement achieved newfound prestige and influence in the 1980s, 1990s, and after. Independent liberal and even radical social problem films, especially in documentary form, made a comeback. Mainstream Hollywood's contribution to the genre continued to present both liberal and conservative views of America's social problems. Spike Lee, the preeminent African American director of this era, addressed racial problems from a politically radical perspective. In *Do the Right Thing* (1989), a disagreement between an Italian pizzeria owner and the poor black residents of New York's Bedford-Stuyvesant neighborhood revealed long-standing frustrations with racial injustice and economic inequality. The movie culminated in violence and sparked significant debate about these issues. Lee's success led to further progressive black filmmaking like John Singleton's *Boyz n the Hood* (1991), as well as more conservative portrayals of African American life. Similarly, women's lives and struggles with sexism were depicted in feminist films such as *Thelma and Louise* (1991) and denigrated in antifeminist, "backlash" films like *Fatal Attraction* (1987). Both films shaped public discussion about gender inequality in American society.

The persistence of the social problem film—even if rarely called that or actually not even "film" but video or digital—into the 21st century came with significant experimentation in subject and style. Andrew deWaard posits the emergence of "the global social problem film" to capture a category or cycle of films about problems with a global reach, such as the international oil market or the War on Terror.[26] A transnational cast of characters depicted in multiple countries characterizes the global social problem film, such as Soderbergh's *Traffic* (2000). Stylistically, these movies often innovate. Complex, multilinear narratives often lack a clear resolution. Realism is not always a priority, and the use of flashy, attention-grabbing cinematography and editing can occur. The 21st-century social problem film focused on domestic issues, like *Crash* (2004), and adopts these cinematic techniques as well. As we have seen in this chapter, genres evolve over time within specific historical and industrial contexts. Understanding what makes the American social problem film a genre and its generic conventions is the topic of our next chapter.

NOTES

1. Kevin Brownlow, *Behind the Mask of Innocence* (New York: Knopf, 1990), xix–xxi.
2. Peter Roffman and Jim Purdy, *The Hollywood Social Problem Film: Madness, Despair and Politics from the Depression to the Fifties* (Bloomington: Indiana University Press, 1981), viii; Steve Neale, *Genre and Hollywood* (London and New York: Routledge, 2000), 45.
3. Roffman and Purdy, *Hollywood Social Problem Film*, 301.
4. Neale, *Genre and Hollywood*, 2.
5. Robert H. Wiebe, *The Search for Order, 1877–1920* (New York: Hill and Wang, 1967).
6. Eileen L. McDonagh, "The 'Welfare Rights State' and the 'Civil Rights State': Policy Paradox and State Building in the Progressive Era," *Studies in American Political Development* 7 (Fall 1993): 225–74.
7. "Edison's Vitascope Cheered," *New York Times*, April 24, 1896, 5.
8. Tom Gunning, "The Cinema of Attractions: Early Film, Its Spectator and the Avant-Garde," rev. and repr. in Thomas Elsaesser, ed., *Early Cinema: Space Frame Narrative* (London: BFI, 1990), 56–62.
9. Kay Sloan, *The Loud Silents: Origins of the Social Problem Film* (Urbana: University of Illinois Press, 1998), 1.
10. Review, *Moving Picture World*, January 13, 1912, quoted in Brownlow, *Behind the Mask of Innocence*, xxi.
11. Steven J. Ross, *Working-Class Hollywood: Silent Film and the Shaping of Class in America* (Princeton, NJ: Princeton University Press, 1998), 55.
12. *Mutual Film Corporation v. Ohio Industrial Commission*, 236 US, 230 US Supreme Court, 1915, 244.
13. Jeanine Basinger, *The Star Machine* (New York: Knopf, 2007).
14. Andrew Bergman, *We're in the Money: Depression America and Its Films* (New York: Harper and Row, 1972), xxi.
15. Roffman and Purdy, *Hollywood Social Problem Film*, x.
16. Steven Mintz and Randy W. Roberts, eds., *Hollywood's America: Twentieth-Century America Through Film*, 4th ed. (Malden, Mass.: Blackwell, 2010), 118–119.
17. Ibid., 219.
18. Thomas Schatz, *Boom and Bust: American Cinema in the 1940s*, vol. 6, Charles Harpole, ed., *History of the American Cinema* (Berkeley: University of California, 1997).
19. Stephen Vaughn, "Political Censorship during the Cold War," in Francis G. Couvares, ed., *Movie Censorship and American Culture* (Washington, DC: Smithsonian Institution Press, 1996), 246.
20. Chris Cagle, *Sociology on Film: Postwar Hollywood's Prestige Commodity* (New Brunswick, NJ: Rutgers University Press, 2017), 126–27.

21. Leighton Grist, *The Films of Martin Scorsese, 1963–77: Authorship and Context* (New York: St. Martin's Press, 2000), 160.
22. Michael Ryan and Douglas Kellner, *Camera Politica: The Politics and Ideology of Contemporary Hollywood Film* (Bloomington: Indiana University Press, 1988), 87.
23. Daniel T. Rogers, *The Age of Fracture* (Cambridge, MA: Harvard University Press, 2011).
24. Geoff King, *New Hollywood Cinema: An Introduction* (repr., London: I. B. Tauris, 2007), 60.
25. "About Us," Sundance Institute website, www.sundance.org/about/us.
26. Andrew deWaard, "The Global Social Problem Film," *Cinephile* 3 (Spring/Summer 2007): 12–18.

WORKS CITED

Basinger, Jeanine. *The Star Machine*. New York: Knopf, 2007.
Bergman, Andrew. *We're in the Money: Depression America and Its Films*. New York: Harper and Row, 1972.
Brownlow, Kevin. *Behind the Mask of Innocence*. New York: Knopf, 1990.
Cagle, Chris. *Sociology on Film: Postwar Hollywood's Prestige Commodity*. New Brunswick, NJ: Rutgers University Press, 2017.
Couvares, Francis G., ed. *Movie Censorship and American Culture*. Washington, DC: Smithsonian Institution Press, 1996.
deWaard, Andrew. "The Global Social Problem Film," *Cinephile* 3 (Spring/Summer 2007): 12–18.
Elsaesser, Thomas, ed. *Early Cinema: Space Frame Narrative*. London: BFI, 1990.
Grist, Leighton. *The Films of Martin Scorsese, 1963–77: Authorship and Context*. New York: St. Martin's Press, 2000.
Gunning, Tom. "The Cinema of Attractions: Early Film, Its Spectator and the Avant-Garde." Rev. and repr. in Thomas Elsaesser, ed., *Early Cinema: Space Frame Narrative*, 56–62. London: BFI, 1990.
King, Geoff. *New Hollywood Cinema: An Introduction*. Repr., London: I. B. Tauris, 2007.
McDonagh, Eileen L. "The 'Welfare Rights State' and the 'Civil Rights State': Policy Paradox and State Building in the Progressive Era." *Studies in American Political Development* 7 (Fall 1993): 225–74.
Mintz, Steven, and Randy W. Roberts, eds., *Hollywood's America: Twentieth-Century America Through Film*, 4th ed. Malden, Mass.: Blackwell, 2010.
Neale, Steve. *Genre and Hollywood*. London and New York: Routledge, 2000.
Roffman, Peter, and Jim Purdy. *The Hollywood Social Problem Film: Madness, Despair and Politics from the Depression to the Fifties*. Bloomington: Indiana University Press, 1981.
Rogers, Daniel T. *The Age of Fracture*. Cambridge, MA: Harvard University Press, 2011.
Ross, Steven J. *Working-Class Hollywood: Silent Film and the Shaping of Class in America*. Princeton, NJ: Princeton University Press, 1998.
Ryan, Michael, and Douglas Kellner. *Camera Politica: The Politics and Ideology of Contemporary Hollywood Film*. Bloomington: Indiana University Press, 1988.
Schatz, Thomas. *Boom and Bust: American Cinema in the 1940s*. Vol. 6, Charles Harpole, ed., *History of the American Cinema*. Berkeley: University of California, 1997.
Sloan, Kay. *The Loud Silents: Origins of the Social Problem Film*. Urbana: University of Illinois Press, 1998.
Vaughn, Stephen. "Political Censorship during the Cold War." In Francis G. Couvares, ed., *Movie Censorship and American Culture*, 237–57. Washington, DC: Smithsonian Institution Press, 1996.
Wiebe, Robert H. *The Search for Order, 1877–1920*. New York: Hill and Wang, 1967.

Chapter Two

Concepts and Conventions of the Social Problem Film

Hollywood has long relied on genres to define and sell its movies. *Genre* is a French word and can be translated into English as "type" or "class." A film genre, then, is a type or class of film. Genre is a way of distinguishing content and style and can be found in literature and drama, as well as film. Genre categories for movies include comedy, drama, musicals, westerns, and science fiction. The number and name of categories can change over time, and subgenres and hybrid genres emerge, like romantic comedies or action thrillers. Motion pictures that fall within each of these categories share distinctive characteristics or conventions. Filmmakers incorporate these conventions, and audiences come to expect them. Like genre categories themselves, these conventions are not static but evolve over time. Such change allows genres to continue to interest artists and appeal to audiences, although too much innovation may prove unsuccessful. Importantly, many individual films do not belong to just one genre but instead cross genres, indicating that genre boundaries are flexible, not rigid.

But who gets to decide what constitutes a genre category and which films fall into it? Genre has been called a critical or—better for our purposes—scholarly invention, developed and used by film scholars to organize their analysis and evaluation of films. Once a genre category is commonly accepted, its defining conventions still are subject to debate. Since the meaning of film is conveyed through both content and style, generic conventions can relate to both. (Although this point too has been debated!) Films within a certain genre "tell familiar stories with familiar characters in familiar situations."[1] A genre's stylistic conventions encompass how the story is told, particularly visually. But sound, setting, and cinematography matter too. Even if generic conventions are agreed upon, whether or not a specific film fits those conventions can be hotly contested. A large body of scholarly literature and genre theory exists and is filled with these discussions and debates.

The social problem film is no exception to these various debates. For some scholars, the social problem film is not even a genre but a cycle of films at a certain historical moment or a series of cycles. For those who agree that it is a genre, its defining conventions and which films fit the category are further debated. But film scholars are not the only contributors to the process of determining and understanding genre. The motion picture industry itself uses genre categories. References to genre can be found during the process of production and distribution. Some filmmakers become associated with a certain genre, either by choice or assignment, and develop talent and expertise in it. Through marketing and exhibition, audiences become familiar with genre categories and develop their favorites. Contemporary reviewers and critics also label and discuss films by genre. As we set out to examine the American social problem film over the 20th and 21st centuries, we will consider scholarly definitions of the genre but also industrial, popular, and critical perspectives. Attention to these perspectives helps to historically contextualize individual social problem films, the genre as a whole, and its conventions.

STARRING ROLE FOR SOCIAL PROBLEMS

The social problem is the subject and even "the star" of these films. The plot is built around the relationship between the characters and the social problem. The protagonist of the movie is confronting it. The protagonist's allies help to ease the problem or the hardships it causes. Rarely do the protagonist and allies actually solve the problem. The antagonist—the enemy of the protagonist—exacerbates the social problem and its adverse consequences or even causes it in the first place. The subject is a contemporary concern, and the story takes place in the present day. That said, as Charles Maland notes, the "lag time between the initial idea for a movie and its completion" can mean a film's ostensible currency is already outmoded by its release date.[2] Even so, we can learn from watching these movies what filmmakers considered the pressing issues of their day. Film reviews from the time will often convey whether critics agreed and offer a sense of the audience's views. *The Best Years of Our Lives* (1946), a film about World War II veterans returning home, received such comment. "Dated? Yes, some people will doubtless call [it] that," while others disagreed, calling the subject "immediately important."[3] None of these sources—producers, reviewers, or spectators—are necessarily correct in their definition of society's ills. How, why, and by whom these come to be seen as "problems" and whether they have an actual basis in social reality reveal much about a film's historical context and conditions.

URGENTLY ADDRESSING THE AUDIENCE

Another convention of the social problem film is its mode of address, which is how a film speaks to and engages the audience. As Peter Roffman and Jim Purdy argue, these films "arouse indignation over some facet of contemporary life."[4] From there, they aim to spur a wish and willingness in filmgoers to resolve these current societal faults. Audiences have to be convinced that the problem is happening now and needs to be targeted immediately. The problem is urgent, harm is being done, and time cannot be wasted. This urgent mode of address appears explicitly in early films and implicitly in later films. Whether silent or sound, movies appearing early on often had an opening title or what later is called a "square-up." This statement introduced and justified—or excused—the subject of the film, defined it as a worthwhile contemporary concern, and called the audience to action.[5] Sometimes a film ended with such a title, and some films offered both. *The Public Enemy* (1931) opened with its aim to "honestly depict an environment that exists today in a certain strata of American life" and closed by naming the "hoodlum" as "a problem that sooner or later WE, the public, must solve." Later films usually made these points through dialogue and plot rather than titles, but they still signaled their status as message movies.

FOSTERING SYMPATHY

This mode of address ideally stirred sympathy or even empathy among filmgoers for the characters on the screen and their counterparts in real life. Maland argues that producers of social problem films were "generally animated by a humane concern for the victim(s) of or crusader(s) against the social problem."[6] They sought to convey that concern and connect to audiences. Amanda Ann Klein considers sympathy "an emotion integral to the effectiveness of the social problem film."[7] Only if audience members invest in and identify with the movie characters and their struggles will the social problem become the filmgoers' concern. This effort to gain sympathy meant many of these films also were melodramas, characterized by emotional excess, and, thus, can be considered a hybrid genre. If sympathy is feeling pity or compassion for someone else, empathy is imagining being in someone else's shoes, facing the same challenges and choices. Film reviews and commentaries from the time often reveal when these feelings were fostered among spectators. When *The Grapes of Wrath* (1940) conveyed the "bitter and terrible" plight of Depression-era migrant farmworkers, a critic believed,

"Insofar as it may stir up a greater sympathy for that plight, it will have accomplished something."[8] Such reactions can tell us spectators' relationship to the problem—close, distant, or nonexistent—and, thus, provide evidence of the relevance of the problem and the film to American society.

DIDACTICISM OR TEACHING A LESSON

A key convention of the social problem film is its didacticism. Roffman and Purdy state that these films "teach a moral lesson of social significance . . . in a didactic fashion."[9] This characteristic puts the genre at odds with mainstream Hollywood's commitment to escapist entertainment. Social problem films still aimed to entertain—after all, they needed to sell tickets—but also to educate. This impulse to inform and instruct shaped the plots, character development, settings, and dialogue of these movies. Over the course of a movie, the protagonist and allies need to learn about the social problem, discover its causes, and determine possible solutions. The audience in the theater gets educated along with the characters onscreen. As a result, these films sometimes were categorized as educational films. While social problem films received compliments for enlightening filmgoers, they also could be criticized for being preachy. The challenge for filmmakers, as Philip Dunne wrote about his screenplay for the racial drama, *Pinky* (1949), was "not to lecture" and "to avoid preaching" but instead "to tell an emotional human story capable of capturing and holding the imagination of the audience." Yet Dunne recognized that not everyone "will find our film either entertaining or edifying."[10] Lessons taught by filmmakers were not always lessons learned by film viewers.

PUBLIC VERSUS PRIVATE PROBLEMS?

Social problem films take on a range of subjects rooted in a variety of social conditions. Some social conditions are considered to be more public in nature, such as poverty and crime, and others are seen as more private, such as family relations and personal health. But the definitions of *public* and *private* differ over time. Better understood as intellectual concepts than actual places, they overlap and interrelate.[11] We see this situation in how social problem films approached their subjects and ascertained causes and solutions. Kay Sloan reflects on these matters with regard to Progressive Era films. "While the cinema suggested that public problems of labor conflict or political corruption could be solved with private romantic solutions, the private conflicts of the domestic sphere required public solutions, such as legislation dealing with temperance, birth control, or prostitution."[12] Considering *The Lost Weekend* (1945), a film released three decades after the Progressive Era,

Chris Cagle similarly conveys the interrelationship between public and private. The problem of alcoholism is portrayed in the film as a personal or individual problem, caused by psychological illness. But the solutions the film also offered—public health and law enforcement—require collective, political action.[13] The relationship between public and private, political and personal, collective and individual presented in social problem films reflected the political ideology of their producers and the popular sociology of their time.

IDEOLOGY AND SOCIOLOGY

Social analysis is a fundamental component of the social problem film. These films examine the problem and explain the causes of it. Contemporary sociological ideas and political ideology play roles in this process, influencing how filmmakers go about their analysis. These films also offer solutions to the problem, and again ideology and sociology matter in determining which solution(s) to a problem a film presents. Liberalism is the political ideology most often associated with the Hollywood social problem film in the 20th century. There is, Maland states, "an implicit assumption that the problem can be treated or even eliminated through well-intentioned liberal social reform."[14] Such liberal films, according to Roffman and Purdy, "present a problem that calls for circumscribed change rather than to call into question some of the deeper values at the foundation of society."[15] Still, conservative and radical or leftist political beliefs and values also have influenced filmmakers working in the genre, as have shifts in sociological thinking over time. Cagle calls the social problem film "a translator of social science into popular culture."[16] When *Home of the Brave* (1949) addressed race prejudice in the US military, it sent the message that a "color-blind," integrated society was best for all Americans, black and white—just as integration came to dominate liberal and sociological thinking on race. Together, politics and sociology shaped how the genre depicted and resolved social problems.

A GENERIC NARRATIVE?

The conventional narrative for a social problem film tells the story in a linear fashion, with a dramatic conflict at the center that is happily resolved at the end. As it turns out, filmmakers often varied and experimented with this convention, and not only in the 21st century. Roffman and Purdy first argued that social problem films fit "the Hollywood Formula," which demanded "a linear narrative with the straightest line of action." "The dramatic conflict was always structured around two opposing poles definitively representing good and evil, with a readily identifiable hero and villain." With the removal of the villain, "a clear-cut, gratifying plot resolution—the Happy Ending" ensues.[17] To achieve this tidy resolution of the narrative, complex social problems, with multiple causes, had to be simplified and personalized. Yet even Roffman and Purdy qualified this convention, admitting that "a surprising number" of social problem films did not fit the formula.[18] Steve Neale strongly concurs, pointing out "the difference, indeed the disjunction, between the resolution of a plot and the resolution of a social problem" common in many films. This disjunction "reminds the viewer that [the proposed solutions] have not (or not yet) actually taken place."[19] As with the closing title of *The Public Enemy*, endings are not always happy. Similarly, an interracial prison escape movie, *The Defiant Ones* (1958), ends with the two men defeated and back behind bars. The "contradictory meanings generated" by these narratives can be seen in contemporary responses to social problem films.[20]

REALISM AS STYLE

Another convention that empowered audiences to draw and express their own meanings from these films is their realistic, visual style. Klein observes that social problem films "emphasized mise-en-scène (and the camera movements that reveal this mise-en-scène) more than any other cinematic element."[21] In shaping the elements of mise-en-scène—all that appears in or frames the cinematic space—filmmakers borrowed visual conventions or "the look" from documentary film. Seeking authenticity, they often filmed on location. Shots of gritty, urban, working-class neighborhoods set the scene for stories about crime or poverty. Even when a movie was filmed in a studio, such settings were re-created. *Dead End* (1937) depicted gangsters and street kids on "a painstaking[ly] detailed set," Klein notes, and the "camera is our omniscient tour guide through the inner city."[22] Along with settings, furnishings, props, costumes, and incidental details were usually contemporaneous and genuine. In this way, the cinematic style of social problem films created the expectation that they were accurate portrayals of the real world. The realism of the style contributed to the "verisimilitude" of the film—that is, the believability of the story—even as filmgoers recognized they were watching a fictional narrative. As representations of a social world, its institutions, and its inhabitants, social problem films can tell us much about their historical time and place.

GENRE AND RECEPTION

These eight conventions encompass the defining characteristics for the genre, but reception also determines genre. The motion picture industry can produce, distribute, and exhibit what it labels a social problem film, but do film reviewers and filmgoers accept the genre category? Does public discussion engage with the movie as a social problem film, whether named as such or not? Recent scholarly definitions of genre privilege reception and discussion. Historian Marnie Hughes-Warrington offers a useful definition of a film's genre: "its location in a timebound network of discussions."[23] Social problem films were generally considered "prestige pictures" within the motion picture industry. Scholar Matthew Bernstein finds they are, in fact, "one of Hollywood's most pretentious and least profitable genres."[24] Yet if timely and relevant, social problem films would be the focus of substantive discussion and debate about the ills and inequalities of American society. They became "sites of discursive practice," in Jason Mittell's words.[25] The issues they raised were always challenging and often controversial. At times, Hollywood filmmakers were accused of exploiting social problems and treating them sensationally to achieve commercial success. Calls for censorship of the genre were issued and even acted upon. In all these ways, public response to social problem films provide a vivid record of social change and conflict in the United States over the 20th century and into the 21st.

NOTES

1. Barry Keith Grant, introduction to Barry Keith Grant, ed., *Film Genre Reader* (Austin, TX: University Press of Austin, 1986), ix.
2. Charles J. Maland, "The Social Problem Film," in Wes D. Gehring, ed., *Handbook of American Film Genres* (Westport, CT: Greenwood Press, 1988), 319.
3. Edwin Schallert, "Best Years of Lives' Saga of Home-Coming," *Los Angeles Times*, December 26, 1946, A3; "Homecoming Soldiers," *New York Times*, December 11, 1946, 30.
4. Peter Roffman and Jim Purdy, *The Hollywood Social Problem Film: Madness, Despair and Politics from the Depression to the Fifties* (Bloomington: Indiana University Press, 1981), 305.
5. Eric Schaefer, *"Bold! Daring! Shocking! True!": A History of Exploitation Films, 1919–1959* (Durham, NC: Duke University Press, 1999), 69–73.
6. Maland, "Social Problem Film," 307.
7. Amanda Ann Klein, *American Film Cycles: Reframing Genres, Screening Social Problems, and Defining Subcultures* (Austin: University of Texas Press, 2011), 82, 86.
8. Edwin Schallert, "'Grapes of Wrath' Due for Much Controversy," *Los Angeles Times*, January 23, 1940, 8.
9. Roffman and Purdy, *Hollywood Social Problem Film*, viii.
10. Philip Dunne, "Approach to Racism: Scenarist of 'Pinky' Explains How Film Will Treat Subject of Negro Prejudice," *New York Times*, May 1, 1949, X5.
11. For an excellent overview, see the *Journal of Women's History* special issues on "Women's History in the New Millennium: Rethinking Public and Private," 15 (Spring 2003), and "Continuing the Conversation," 15 (Summer 2003).
12. Kay Sloan, *The Loud Silents: Origins of the Social Problem Film* (Urbana: University of Illinois Press, 1998), 80.
13. Chris Cagle, *Sociology on Film: Postwar Hollywood's Prestige Commodity* (New Brunswick, NJ: Rutgers University Press, 2017), 46.
14. Maland, "Social Problem Film," 307.
15. Roffman and Purdy, *Hollywood Social Problem Film*, 269.

16. Cagle, *Sociology on Film*, 7.
17. Roffman and Purdy, *Hollywood Social Problem Film*, 4–5.
18. Ibid., 7.
19. Steve Neale, *Genre and Hollywood* (London and New York: Routledge, 2000), 115.
20. Marcia Landy, *British Genres: Cinema and Society, 1930–1960* (Princeton, NJ: Princeton University Press, 1991), 436–37.
21. Klein, *American Film Cycles*, 63.
22. Ibid., 63–64.
23. Marnie Hughes-Warrington, *History Goes to the Movies: Studying History on Film* (New York: Routledge, 2007), 191.
24. Matthew Bernstein, *Walter Wanger: Hollywood Independent* (Berkeley: University of California Press, 1994), 394.
25. Jason Mittell, "A Cultural Approach to Television Genre Theory," *Cinema Journal* 40 (Spring 2001): 9.

WORKS CITED

Bernstein, Matthew. *Walter Wanger: Hollywood Independent*. Berkeley: University of California Press, 1994.
Cagle, Chris. *Sociology on Film: Postwar Hollywood's Prestige Commodity*. New Brunswick, NJ: Rutgers University Press, 2017.
Gehring, Wes D. *Handbook of American Film Genres*. Westport, CT: Greenwood Press, 1988.
Grant, Barry Keith, ed. *Film Genre Reader*. Austin, TX: University Press of Austin, 1986.
Hughes-Warrington, Marnie. *History Goes to the Movies: Studying History on Film*. New York: Routledge, 2007.
Klein, Amanda Ann. *American Film Cycles: Reframing Genres, Screening Social Problems, and Defining Subcultures*. Austin: University of Texas Press, 2011.
Landy, Marcia. *British Genres: Cinema and Society, 1930–1960*. Princeton, NJ: Princeton University Press, 1991.
Maland, Charles J. "The Social Problem Film." In Wes D. Gehring, ed., *Handbook of American Film Genres*, 305–30. Westport, CT: Greenwood Press, 1988.
Mittell, Jason. "A Cultural Approach to Television Genre Theory." *Cinema Journal* 40 (Spring 2001): 3–24.
Neale, Steve. *Genre and Hollywood*. London and New York: Routledge, 2000.
Roffman, Peter, and Jim Purdy. *The Hollywood Social Problem Film: Madness, Despair and Politics from the Depression to the Fifties*. Bloomington: Indiana University Press, 1981.
Schaefer, Eric. *"Bold! Daring! Shocking! True!": A History of Exploitation Films, 1919–1959*. Durham, NC: Duke University Press, 1999.
Sloan, Kay. *The Loud Silents: Origins of the Social Problem Film*. Urbana: University of Illinois Press, 1998.

TOPICS OVER TIME

Chapter Three

Labor and Class Conflict, according to Hollywood

As Chris Cagle has pointed out, "we now have sufficient historical distance" to examine social problem films more fully as we continually strive to grasp the complexity of "cultural undercurrents" of another time from our own.[1] Only recently have books like Cagle's begun to treat these films on their own ideological terms, engaging in a more systematic analysis of the genre's complexity. There will certainly be more academic analyses to follow, and many more social problem films will emerge in the coming years as deserving serious scholarly treatment. In the meantime, this chapter takes a different approach, attempting to lay out what that systematic analysis would look like when you are the one examining labor and class conflict social problem films not discussed in this chapter.

Most analysis attempts to solve some kind of problem, but the scholars who do this well frequently make the process look intuitive and seamless. Yet no one is born having these skills. You learn them as a result of years of advanced training. You need not earn a PhD to grasp the basic principles of the process. Rather than assume you will intuitively grasp the series of steps scholars use to solve academic problems, to better understand the workings of social problem films treating labor and class conflict, this chapter uses that subgroup of social problems as the vehicle to better understand the process itself. That process, when done effectively, works equally well when analyzing other kinds of social problem films, musicals, newsreels, or any other genre or media format, for that matter.

The basic process for solving academic problems has evolved over hundreds of years and consists of a series of steps. When strung together, these steps frequently comprise the basic outline of a solid research paper. However, in practice, any one of these steps can work autonomously and in isolation from one another too, and they make for good pedagogy. Much of academic practice, for example, involves finding the right kind of academic problem for which there is a solution. It involves being able to convince a skeptical community why they should care about the problem. It involves building arguments, informed by existing scholarship. It involves bringing evidence to bear in the solving of problems. Any one of these practices should be an integral part of any educational enterprise, whether at the high school or college level. Rarefied academic debates do not have the corner on the practices of making good scholarly arguments, informed by evidence. Being able to do this well is the cornerstone of any democracy, which functions only as well as its democratic institutions can yield informed citizens, who sometimes have to make difficult political and cultural decisions. Such practices should be as much at home in the college classroom as they should reside in the high school classroom, practiced equally and fully by both teachers and students alike. Any one of the steps described below can, in isolation, make for a classroom discussion or exercise. Strung together, these steps guide a high school term paper just as well as they guide a doctoral dissertation.

SOCIAL PROBLEMS AND SCHOLARLY PROBLEMS

Both social problem films and scholarship attempt to tackle problems, though the kinds of problems each try to solve, and how they go about solving them, remain very different. At the turn of the last century, short films such as *Children Who Labor* (1912) or *Cry of the Children* (1912) exposed film audiences to the social problem of child labor. With the rise of mechanization, mass industrialization, assembly-line methods of mass production, as well as a rise in consumerism to meet demand for mass-produced goods, child labor could help an impoverished family make ends meet. At the same time, it satisfied economies of scale by ensuring manufacturers could pay as little as possible for the labor necessary to keep production going. Of course, cheap labor meant having 12-year-olds working in coal mines, 11-year-olds working in the mills, and 5-year-olds picking shrimp, as documented in the photography of sociologist Lewis Hine. In 1904, the National Child Labor Committee (NCLC) formed to advocate for both mandatory public education and abolition of all child labor. Not until the Fair Labor Standards Act (FLSA) in 1938 did Congress pass legislation prohibiting the most egregious abuses of child labor and that could withstand the many challenges that previous attempts at legislation had faced in the courts.

What problem or problems were *Children Who Labor* and *Cry of the Children* trying to solve, and how do we know whether they were ultimately successful? Going on just the quarter century alone that it took between the screening of these films and the passage of any legislation meaningfully outlawing the practice, one might glibly conclude that the films were not very successful in solving the problem of child labor in the United States. According to Zama Coursen-Neff, the deputy director of the Children's Rights Division of the Human Rights Watch, hundreds of thousands of children in the United States still toil long hours under agribusiness's harsh and frequently hazardous working conditions.[2] But to say that these two short films, in and of themselves, would solve the entire problem of child labor in the United States seems a great deal more naive than anything the filmmakers hoped to accomplish in making a film about the problem. Perhaps their goal was simply to raise awareness of the issue or to exert public pressure on opinion makers. Or perhaps they simply wanted to educate audiences on the problem and potential solutions and, without dictating any one solution, let the public decide.

Like social problem films, academic essays also attempt to solve problems. And like social problem films, if the yardstick we use to judge their success ultimately depends on whether they actually solve social problems, academic essays will fail, miserably. But then, it is the yardstick we use to measure success, as opposed to the film or essay, that may be the problem. By choosing to write about *Children Who Labor* or *Cry of the Children*, you probably would want to solve a problem related to our knowledge or understanding of what those films were doing or not doing. But you likely would not solve the problem of child labor by choosing to write about a film depicting the subject. And yet your unique insight or understanding of those films can help contribute to a broader understanding of cultural attitudes toward child labor. Or perhaps make us see something more clearly about why it took a quarter of a century before there was court-proof legislation banning child labor. Or perhaps help us to understand why horrific abuses of child labor continue to take place today, not just in some remote foreign dictatorship but in the United States.

Solving academic problems, like solving social problems, does not happen in one fell swoop. Rather, solutions occur because of a series of well-honed and sometimes arduous smaller steps. In the case of academic study, scholars have honed these steps over centuries. Think of how the many steps many took to eradicate the prevalence of child labor in the United States. People who cared about this issue got together and formed the NCLC. The organization helped the Edison Company produce *Children Who Labor*. The NCLC published Hine's photos in newspapers and magazines, and sponsored public exhibitions incorporating his slides. The organization supported numerous attempts at legislation before the FLSA in 1938. Each one of these steps occurred as a result of work that built on the efforts of others and on the dedicated work of a community of people who fought and cared passionately about this issue over a period of decades. Many aspects of this struggle could characterize how scholarship solves problems too. An individual scholar first identifies a problem to solve that he or she cares deeply about. That scholar then seeks out a community of like-minded individuals who also share that concern. The community dismantles the problem into a series of smaller or more manageable chunks to solve. Rather than reinvent the wheel, they figure out how to build upon one another's efforts and achieve some momentum, working in concert with one another. They come up with arguments to advance their cause and accumulate mounting evidence to support those arguments. Ultimately, and through a lot of trial, error, and even abject failure, something changes—eventually—because of sustained and coordinated thinking and effort on the part of a group of dedicated and like-minded people.

The good news is that for most academic problems, including those related to our knowledge of film and media, many people have already laid some important groundwork necessary for a solution. A key part of your job as a student or as a teacher will be to figure out what already has been done, how you can build upon it, and how your research adds to this preexisting knowledge and can still make a meaningful contribution to the scholarship. The steps one would take for putting together a research paper on the history of child labor would be fairly similar to the steps one would take for putting together a research paper about a historical film depicting child labor.

- First, you would identify a problem involving the film.
- Second, you would explain why that problem should matter to someone other than just you.
- Third, you would propose an overriding idea that, as you develop it with other ideas and evidence, will contribute something toward solving the problem you identified. Perhaps the problem might be something that we don't know or that we think we know but actually don't know well enough.
- Fourth, you explain how, rather than reinventing the wheel, your work builds upon the work of a community of scholars who have laid the groundwork for your research to occur.
- Fifth, you work to advance your overriding idea with a series of smaller ideas, which you try to preview as much as possible early in the paper.
- Sixth, you offer evidence to support these claims.
- And seventh, you explain what has changed or will change as a result of the scholarship you contribute to a community of people who care about the subject. And if you're feeling really generous, you might suggest new problems that have emerged as a result of your research. Maybe in the process, you realized there are other things we don't know or don't know well enough. Someone else then can pick up where you left off. Or what has changed may lead you to a new research direction.

Early on in the process, you first should be able to define a problem your research is trying to solve in academic terms. According to Wayne Booth, we define academic problems either in terms of a gap in existing knowledge or as a way to strengthen knowledge about something we think we already have. If we return to our early examples of *Children Who Labor* and *Cry of the Children*, for example, we might conclude, after a survey of existing scholarship on these films, that we really don't have a very good understanding of what the filmmakers actually hoped to accomplish in the making of these films. If you draw this conclusion from existing scholarship about these films, then you need to make a case for why this problem would matter to other people interested in films about child labor or perhaps more generally about social problem films. As we've already mentioned, perhaps better understanding of what the filmmakers hoped to accomplish by making a film would tell us something about broader cultural attitudes toward child labor at the time. Or perhaps we should care about how well we understand the filmmakers' objectives, because that understanding could help yield greater insight into the struggle to outlaw child labor. Or maybe this understanding matters because however noble the sentiments were in making these films at the time, we still haven't figured out effective strategies to combat child labor today.

Establishing the significance of the problem is an essential step in building an argument and one you should be able to demonstrate as mattering, not just to you personally but to a community of other scholars who might also be interested in the topic, and even contributing to a solution. Any number of Hollywood and independent films today make some kind of reference to labor and class conflict issues. Why should you care about *The Passaic Textile Strike*, a 1926 American silent film produced by the Communist Party and the International Workers' Aid to help raise funds in support of 15,000 workers in New Jersey who went on strike to protest their horrific working conditions? As it turns out, many believed the complete film lost until 2006, when New York University's Tamiment Library acquired the papers of the US Community Party and discovered a complete print of the film within the collection. Not only did these rediscovered reels feature important documentary footage long thought lost forever; the 1926 film itself is one of the earliest films still in existence to feature labor issues sympathetically from the perspective of the working class.

Once you've established the significance of studying a film like *The Passaic Textile Strike*, a part of which now is available online from the Internet Film Archive, your next step would be to establish a central premise or overriding idea to develop over the course of your paper or project. In *Working-Class Hollywood: Silent Film and the Shaping of Class in America*, Steven J. Ross argues that *The Passaic Textile Strike* was one of a handful of films from the 1920s that "contested Hollywood representations of contemporary labor struggles and offered audiences markedly different ways of understanding and resolving class conflict."[3] If we trace Ross's argument further, we might examine how he uses evidence and supporting points to show in what ways the film could contest existing representations and what kinds of alternatives these representations could offer. We might then try to test or poke holes in this thesis. Do newspaper reviews of the time bear out the close reading Ross performed on the film? Are there other Hollywood films that more closely parallel what *The Passaic Textile Strike* is doing than Ross's argument would have you believe? Any one of these premises could lead to an overriding idea for your own research project. And whether what you find ultimately confirms or departs from Ross's original thesis hardly matters. Either way, your project still will make a valuable contribution. Either the work you contribute validates Ross's thesis and points to other aspects of the film to test or if you find significant new information, your work opens up a new path to discovery.

Testing a central premise or overriding idea doesn't have to be particularly ambitious or complicated. Lots of films depict some aspect of labor and class conflict. Does having some aspect of the film devoted to labor and class conflict automatically make the film a social problem film? Charlie Chaplin's *Modern Times* (1936), for example, satirizes industrialization and the regimentation of modern life under capitalism. But the film also is a comedy, a romance, and perhaps most importantly, a Chaplin film. Chaplin himself wrote, directed, edited, scored, and starred in his own film. He also owned the studio that produced it, which was probably the only way such a film would ever get made in Hollywood. At what point do we decide that *Modern Times* matches enough attributes of the genre that it operates as a social problem film? There are documentaries, newsreels, animated shorts, and foreign films that all might address labor and class conflict issues. But they do not meet some basic criteria. They are not feature-length films. Or, in the case of foreign films, they were not produced by a Hollywood studio. We might look to another genre, perhaps a western or a biographical picture. Warren Beatty's historical biopic *Reds* (1982), for example, depicted John Reed's involvement with the Russian Revolution. But as a historical biopic and a romance, it displaces some of the urgency and present tense we might expect of a social problem film. One might ultimately conclude that the slapstick sequences of *Modern Times* similarly displace any serious point the film would make with regard to labor and class conflict. Yet a close viewing of the film might reveal that the film's comedy actually makes serious points about labor and class conflict and beseeches us to find a solution to the problems it identifies, in line with what other social problem films were doing at the time. Again, either way, pursuing the question of whether *Modern Times* behaves like a social problem film would make a contribution to the scholarship. *Modern Times* has received a great deal of scholarly attention, but only a few books and scholarly essays seriously take up a discussion of how the film behaves within the parameters of the social problem film genre.

HOW WELL DO WE UNDERSTAND SOCIAL PROBLEM FILMS ABOUT LABOR AND CLASS CONFLICT?

Were we to proceed with the overriding premise that Chaplin's satirical comedy does behave according to the conventions of the social problem film, even though it diverges significantly from the dramatic mode of other social problem films, then the next step would be to show where either gaps or weaknesses in our understanding already exist. However, we also want to demonstrate where there are significant parallels—or departures—in basic assumptions. Demonstrating gaps and weaknesses and parallels in assumptions outwardly helps save some time so that we are not having to reinvent the wheel or redo work others already have accomplished. But more meaningfully, scholarly writing is always done in collaboration. Even if you never meet anyone else writing about *Modern Times* or social problem films face-to-face, you have something unique to say about that film. Your thinking, your opinions, and your research can make a contribution to a community out there that may have a deep interest in these topics. You can join this community and make a meaningful contribution to it by helping to identify gaps and weaknesses in the scholarship that already exists about social problem films that depict labor and class conflict.

How do you go about making a case that our existing understanding of *Modern Times* has gaps and weaknesses? Chaplin's film is a classic, so plenty of academic writing on it already exists. You could try to find a few representative examples of essays and books that talk about *Modern Times* but never mention the social problem film. You also could find all of the scholarship that exists on social problem films depicting labor and class conflict and show how they never mention Chaplin's film. These are good first steps, but you also can be more creative in demonstrating either a gap or weakness in our understanding of this film in particular or a gap or weakness in our understanding of the social problem film more generally. One question to ask is whether there are *other* films of that era that depart from the social problem film's typical dramatic mode but that otherwise engage the genre's conventions in depicting labor and class conflict. In *Blackface, White Noise*, scholar Michael Rogin argues that Warner Bros. Depression-era musical comedies like *Gold Diggers of 1933* and *42nd Street* "made music out of social problems," with *Gold Diggers* "a deliberate New Deal parable" featuring an elaborate but foreboding final "production number, 'My Forgotten Man,' that evoked in name an FDR campaign speech and in sound and image the bonus marchers on Washington."[4] Rogin doesn't go into much depth regarding how these musicals "made music out of social problems," but he does establish some groundwork for you to make an argument that not every social problem film dealing with labor and class conflict used a dramatic mode. Your line of reasoning then could develop the idea that there is a gap in the scholarship concerning "hybrid" social problem films. Or that the scholarship might lead us to believe we think we know how musicals and comedies treat labor and class conflict, but in fact understanding what the social problem film is doing helps us to better understand how films like *Modern Times* actually operate.

In addition to using other scholarship to show gaps or weaknesses in knowledge about social problem films that address labor and class conflict—gaps and weaknesses that your thinking and analysis about a particular topic will address—you will want to show significant parallels in or departures from assumptions. In his discussion of social problem films, for example, genre scholar Steve Neale acknowledged a central idea of Peter Roffman and Jim Purdy, the "Formula" that the latter scholars argued governed Hollywood social problem films: linear plot lines with goal-oriented protagonists, dramatic conflict with identifiable villains, recognizable stars, and continuity and reproducibility between similar film groupings within a genre. Neale accepted much of this central formula in his discussion of the social problem film.[5] After all, the underlying premise that we can group different kinds of films according to genres would assume that there is some kind of reproducible formula at work that allows us to create groupings of films in the first place. But Neale noted that even Roffman and Purdy had to account for "industrially exceptional" films in the social problem film genre, like Chaplin's *Modern Times*. Neale used this point to argue that even "less obviously exceptional" social problem films like *The Grapes of Wrath* (1940) notably lack one or more of the genre's formulaic features. *The Grapes of Wrath*, an adaptation of a celebrated and controversial John Steinbeck novel, lacked a clear-cut villain. The film follows the fictional Joad family, after losing their farm to a bank foreclosure, as they move to California and struggle to find shelter and employment during the height of the Great Depression. "When the Joads are tractored off their land," observed Neale, "Muley (John Qualen) asks 'Who do I shoot?' It is part of the point that there is no clear-cut or obvious answer."[6]

In the process of developing Roffman and Purdy's notion of the "Formula," Neale contributed some nuance and refinement to it in identifying what he considered a key feature of the social problem film: a disjunction. Neale's improvement upon Roffman and Purdy's idea allowed him to note that social problem films frequently feature the disjunction "between the resolution of a plot and the resolution of a social problem, something commentators on social problem films often ignore. Disjunctions like this are very common in social problem films, which tend as a rule to insist that the problems they deal with are *not* resolved, and which replace the possible resolution of social problems with the actual resolution of personal ones."[7]

Were we to develop Neale's concept of disjunction, we might want to test it with a different film. Does the disparity between plot resolution and social problem resolution apply to the independently produced *Salt of the Earth* (1954), a docudrama shot on location reenacting the Empire Zinc Company strike in New Mexico, with many of the Mexican American miners who had participated in the strike? The film is somewhat unique. Made at the height of the anti-Communist McCarthy era, it employed numerous creative talents that Hollywood had blacklisted from working in the major studios. Hollywood studios joined the US House of Representatives, the Federal Bureau of Investigation, the American Legion, and other organizations in banning *Salt of the Earth* from processing labs and theater screenings across the country.

Despite being made outside the Hollywood studio system and being made into a cultural pariah of Hollywood, *Salt of the Earth* is a conventional social problem film by the standards of the genre. It focuses in particular on one Mexican American family as the protagonists. Unlike *The Grapes of Wrath*, there are identifiable villains: the mine owners and the sheriff who ends up enforcing the Taft-Hartley Act to break up the strike. The act, passed in 1947 as the Labor Management Relations Act, severely curtailed labor unions' ability to mobilize strikes and engage in political speech. The film's actual resolution occurs once the wives of the miners organize to take over the strike from their husbands. Yet in depicting this victory, the film opens up a new frontier of social problems. Despite the injustices and inequality perpetrated upon them, the Chicano miners fail to see the injustices and inequality they themselves perpetrate upon the women in their families. Were we to develop Neale's idea further, we might want to argue that unlike other social problem films, *Salt of the Earth* offers a disjunction between the actual resolution of one social problem, a labor conflict, and the film's unresolved social problem of sexism and unequal rights for Chicana women in that working-class community. There is a parallel in understanding this theory of how genres work, and yet the application of this theory to *Salt of the Earth* is different enough from Neale's original description to fill a gap in our understanding, both about how this film works specifically and perhaps also for social problem films in general. In this way, we build upon Neale's original work, carve out a niche to talk about *Salt of the Earth* in a way that hasn't yet occurred, and at the same time create new opportunities for others to test different films and see if the theory would apply to them.

BREAKING DOWN AND DEVELOPING YOUR MAIN IDEA

Once you've used existing scholarship on the social problem film to show how your ideas both build upon and contribute to our understanding of the labor and class conflict social problem film, you can develop an overriding premise or idea by breaking it down into smaller chunks. Suppose we took another social problem film about labor and class conflict from 1954, *On the Waterfront*. And suppose we wanted to test whether the idea of disjunction between the actual resolution of one social problem and the lack of resolution of another unresolved social problem might help us understand a film clearly made within the Hollywood studio system. *On the Waterfront* depicts a variety of social problems: labor and working conditions, union corruption, crime, the role of the individual against the powers that be, poverty, the city, the relevance of religion in confronting modern-day problems. Marlon Brando plays Terry Molloy, an outsider dockworker who goes up against the labor union machine that controls the loading and unloading of cargo off the ships in the harbor. The film won eight Oscars, including Best Picture, Best Director, Best Actor for Brando, and Best Supporting Actress for Eva Marie Saint, who plays Molloy's love interest. Were we to test the idea of disjunction, we might find it "less obviously exceptional" than a film like *Salt of the Earth* or *Modern Times*. The film is a straightforward drama with identifiable villains, the corrupt union bosses. It has a love interest. It also ends with the protagonist standing up to the antagonists in a violent conflict and a resolution that involves a victory of the little guy over the bullies.

Despite the film justly being celebrated, it also is not without controversy. Many of the people involved with the making of the film were in real life informers who cooperated with the US House Un-American Activities Committee (HUAC), which throughout the 1950s investigated so-called subversive activity in American life, including in Hollywood. HUAC pressured studios to ban *Salt of the Earth* and create blacklists preventing left-leaning artists from working within the industry. Many struggled to find work, using pseudonyms or fronts. Some had to leave the country. Others committed suicide. Persecuting artists because of their political beliefs was one of the darker chapters in American history. Key to how the blacklist worked, the committee would subpoena a witness. All Congress had to do was suspect you of holding Communist beliefs. Or perhaps you had a friend or family member who Congress suspected of harboring Communist sympathies. If you refused to cooperate with the committee, you were an unfriendly witness and you were put on a blacklist. If, however, you were willing to cooperate with the committee, you could get off or stay off a blacklist by admitting guilt and naming names of other friends and colleagues who you suspected had Communist leanings.

Many believe *On the Waterfront* used labor and class conflict in its narrative as a metaphor to justify cooperation by some who were involved in the making of the film and who themselves named names for HUAC. Victor Navasky argued in *Naming Names* that *On the Waterfront* "makes the definitive case for the HUAC informer or at least is—among its considerable other achievements—a valiant attempt to complicate the public perception of the issue."[8] Were we to develop this idea, we might discuss the disjunction between the explicit resolution of the social problem of labor and union corruption and the implicit social problem of anti-Communism and the ethics of informing. Note that this idea narrowed down the number of social problems to discuss. Don't forget that *On the Waterfront* deals with many social problems, but we don't necessarily want to write an entire book about the film. Still, the disjunction between an explicit and implicit social problem is broad, and we would want to break down this idea further.

Navasky developed the idea that *On the Waterfront* could serve as a kind of allegory for 1950s anti-Communism by further breaking down this argument in terms of the evidence at hand: a discussion of the film's narrative; what the film's director, Elia Kazan, has had to say about his work; and a quick survey of themes from Kazan's other film and literary output. For example, Navasky used very specific examples of dialogue and basic plot lines of the film to illustrate the larger point:

> The movie is rife with talk of "rats," "stoolies," "cheesies," "canaries." Terry Malloy has to choose between the waterfront ethic, which holds ratting to be the greatest evil, and the Christian ethic, which suggests that one ought to speak truth to power. The former is represented by the vulgar, vicious, cigar-chomping corrupt labor boss, Johnny Friendly (Lee J. Cobb, also a real-life informer), and the latter by the clean-cut, gutsy, straight-talking priest, Father Barry (Karl Malden). Terry comes to maturity and wins the girl (Eva Marie Saint) when he gains the courage to inform. In addition he achieves heroic stature as he single-handedly takes on the mob at the risk of his life and in the process comes to true self-knowledge. "I been ratting on myself all these years," he tells Johnny Friendly, "and I didn't know it. I'm glad what I done."[9]

Navasky then developed this idea further by discussing some interviews Kazan gave where he justified his decision to cooperate with HUAC and by examining how themes of informing occur in Kazan's other works. However, there are other kinds of filmic and nonfilmic evidence we might use to examine the labor and class conflict social problem film closely.

FILMIC AND NONFILMIC EVIDENCE OF THE LABOR AND CLASS CONFLICT SOCIAL PROBLEM FILM

In thinking about the labor and class conflict social problem film, we want to draw upon as much evidence, and as many different kinds of evidence, as possible. In his reading of *On the Waterfront*, Navasky drew from repeated close viewings of the film to connect the script's dialogue to broader questions about the ethics of informing. At the same time, and perhaps to guard against accusations that it was just his particular reading of the film or that he was reading too much into the film, he gathered other evidence. Some of that evidence involved Kazan's other films. But most of the evidence involved nonfilmic evidence, such as Kazan's writings or interviews he gave. Robert Allen and Douglas Gomery note that "nonfilmic materials prove invaluable," and often simply closely studying a film alone "is really an inappropriate research method."[10] Note here that in terms of close viewings, as well as with evidence closely related in time and place to the film itself, we are talking about primary evidence of the object at hand. In this case, we would be discussing the film itself, production records related to the film, or eyewitness accounts by those involved with the making of the film. This evidence would differ from academic analysis of social problem films, almost always once removed from the actual object of study, like those of Navasky, Neale, or Roffman and Purdy. In regard to discussions involving the social problem film, we generally would consider those secondary sources.

Were we to test the idea of a disjunction between *On the Waterfront*'s ostensible and explicit social problem involving labor union corruption and its implicit and unresolved social problem involving the ethics of informing during the McCarthy era, what other kinds of nonfilmic primary evidence could we use? We could try to find newspaper reviews and columns of the time to see if any critics picked up on this tension as well. In her regular column on Hollywood, Hedda Hopper included an item on the film in 1954. Going in to see the film, Hopper "kept looking for a message since [actor Lee J.] Cobb, Elia Kazan . . . and Budd Schulberg, who wrote it, were all up before the un-American activities committee." Interestingly, though, Hopper denied that there was any connection, arguing "the only message is against crime and evil."[11] However, we should be careful not to take Hooper at face value. Perhaps some who were advocating on behalf of anti-Communism saw political value or advantage in insisting that the film was only about crime and evil, and denying the film's politics was attempting to apologize or explain away the filmmakers' controversial politics or actions outside the soundstage.

Because labor and class conflict social problem films so often serve as lightning rods for subjects other than issues related to labor and class conflict—perhaps a characteristic of the subgenre worthy of its own study—

nonfilmic materials become essential to understanding not only how the film made sense in its particular time and place but also how the film made sense to particular audiences in a particular time and space. *Norma Rae* (1979), a biopic based on an actual unionization effort that took place at a North Carolina textile mill, will probably be better remembered for being about the real-life Crystal Lee Sutton, on whom actress Sally Field's performance is based. Sutton reportedly did not like the film. Field won the 1985 Academy Award for her performance in another film. In her acceptance speech for that film, she invoked dialogue from her character in *Norma Rae*, admitting that "you like me, right now, you like me!" The moment became a kind of cultural catchphrase for gushing celebrity self-absorption, with Field even parodying herself in a 2015 Charles Schwab commercial.

To explain the way in which a star's performance can eclipse the actual person who served as the basis of the performance, we might turn to Richard DeCordova's concept of the star as "a specific path of intertextuality that extends outside of the text as a formal system."[12] By "intertextuality," DeCordova means simply the relationship of one text—for example, an individual film like *Norma Rae*—with another. In the case of a star text of Sally Field, we might look to her many appearances outside her performance in *Norma Rae*: her Academy Award acceptance speech, her self-parody in a Charles Schwab commercial, and the like. We might ask what cultural forces or processes are at work that would dislocate the film's attempt at an authentic representation of a labor organizer, making one of these details a punch line for an investment banking firm commercial, and completely sever the ties of that reference from the actual person with whom that dialogue purportedly originated. The star text—in this case, the various elements related to Field's performance in *Norma Rae*—make up but one intertext running through a film originally about labor struggle and class conflict. But there are other intertexts between filmic and nonfilmic evidence that might help us better understand the reception of the film.

Newspapers frequently serve as both an accessible and valuable source of nonfilmic evidence. That evidence features important background information you might not get from watching the film alone. Such evidence also helps us understand the interconnections and interplay that exists between film and other media. A profile of *Norma Rae*'s director, Martin Ritt, appeared in the *New York Times* before the film was set to open. Ritt, who had worked under director Elia Kazan throughout the 1930s as part of the New York–based Group Theatre company, later found himself the subject of anti-Communist blacklists. The newspaper profile, written by reporter Aljean Harmetz, frames Ritt's involvement in *Norma Rae* in terms of his political sensibilities, which the article asserts are a commitment to liberalism rather than Communism. That liberalism appeals to more universal aspects of the human condition. "I'm an urban Jew," Ritt told Harmetz. "But I'm as

American as apple pie or chopped liver. I've always felt related to rural America. I like the pace of the rural South and Southwest, the work of it, the fair shake of it. The people are tough and funny. The heart of *Norma Rae* is . . . affirmation about struggle."[13]

In addition to helping universalize the appeal of *Norma Rae* by generalizing "labor strife" to encompass affirmations of struggle and breaking down barriers between rural apple pie and urban chopped liver, the article gives us some valuable information about the role that newspapers themselves can play in getting a film made. Ritt had first read about Crystal Lee Sutton, the subject of the film, in a *New York Times Magazine* article by Henry P. Leiferman.[14] The intertext between the newspaper and the film not only becomes a way of promoting the film but a way of helping to shape audience expectations of how the film will depict labor strife in terms of "affirmation of struggle." The newspaper report became the genesis for the making of the film itself.

WHAT'S CHANGED AS A RESULT OF STUDYING LABOR AND CLASS CONFLICT SOCIAL PROBLEM FILMS?

The seventh and final step in any academic inquiry involves looking at what has changed as a result of your examination, in this case of labor and class conflict social problems. This chapter has attempted to show how a systematic process of academic inquiry and problem solving can help us better understand social problem films that address labor and class conflict. The solution academic inquiry provides is not one that solves problems of labor inequality or class conflict. Rather, the solution tells us something about how the films themselves work culturally or how the individuals and organizations involved understood—or perhaps misunderstood—their role in the context of a broader struggle. Deeper understanding today of how these films were effective or ineffective might help craft better campaigns in the future, one where child labor and hazardous working conditions don't appear to be going away anytime soon.

When put together, these steps comprise a research paper. But the steps work equally well in isolation from one another. Both teachers and students can engage with any one of them and build a classroom exercise around it. For example, we could test the idea of the labor and social conflict intertext by looking for evidence of the role investigative reporting played in another film depicting a central working-class heroine, *North Country* (2005). Did newspapers play a role in the genesis of that film, the way they played a role in the making of *Norma Rae*? This exercise could involve asking the class to come up with other examples of labor and class conflict films "based on a true story." This could lead to a discussion of where "true stories" come from and how films capitalize on them. But this step also could involve more preparation outside of class. A teacher could have students read the *New York Times*' original profile of Crystal Lee Sutton and prepare a clip from *Norma Rae* to screen in class. Both comprise evidence, but what are the relationships between nonfilmic and filmic evidence? What do those relationships tell us about the interplay between texts and how audiences can create meanings?

Because this chapter has set out a series of steps to better understand labor and class conflict social problem films, where each step works as well autonomously as it does as part of a larger process, there is still a lot of ground we haven't covered. We haven't delved particularly deeply into any of the films discussed. There is a growing body of scholarship on the labor and class conflict social problem film that the chapter did not include. Remember, the discussion of secondary literature is not meant to be exhaustive but, as representative, a means to an end. The chapter has built an argument about using the steps in the process of academic inquiry to identify gaps in knowledge and weaknesses in understanding. The next steps would involve others identifying films not mentioned here that would fit the profile of the labor and class conflict social problem film. Many of these films have generated their own scholarly articles and even books, some specifically addressing a single title.

Finally, this chapter has opened up new areas of inquiry outside of the labor and class conflict social problem film. Many of the films discussed in this chapter are not just about labor or class conflict. All of them are about labor or class conflict plus something else. Many have chosen to read the dockworker strike depicted in *On the Waterfront* as a metaphor for the act of informing during Congress's investigation of supposed Communist influences in Hollywood. The film's narrative also is as much about organized crime and corruption as it is about labor. *Salt of the Earth* isn't just about a miner strike. It engages issues of race and gender as well. No single chapter can adequately address all of these issues and connections. But subsequent chapters in this book will place more emphasis on how the social problem film engages these other issues as well. Ultimately, though, your thinking and writing that goes beyond the chapter, building upon the work of others, identifying the gaps, and refining and revising what we think we already know are the only guarantees that we will ever come close to grasping what the labor and class conflict social problem film truly is doing.

NOTES

1. Chris Cagle, *Sociology on Film: Postwar Hollywood's Prestige Commodity* (New Brunswick, NJ: Rutgers University Press, 2017), 6.
2. Zama Coursen-Neff, "Child Farmworkers in the United States: A 'Worst Form of Child Labor,'" Human Rights Watch website, November 17, 2011, accessed August 1, 2017, www.hrw.org/news/2011/11/17/child-farmworkers-united-states-worst-form-child-labor.

3. Steven J. Ross, *Working-Class Hollywood* (1998): 143.
4. Michael Rogin, *Blackface, White Noise: Jewish Immigrants in the Hollywood Melting Pot* (Berkeley: University of California Press, 1996), 167.
5. Steve Neale, *Genre and Hollywood* (London: Routledge-Taylor and Francis, 2005), 114.
6. Ibid., 115.
7. Ibid., 115–16; original emphasis.
8. Victor S. Navasky, *Naming Names* (New York: Penguin, 1982), 209.
9. Ibid., 209.
10. Robert C. Allen and Douglas Gomery, *Film History: Theory and Practice* (Boston: McGraw-Hill, 1985), 38.
11. Hedda Hopper, "Looking at Hollywood: Story of Levi Pants and How They Grew to Be Told in Film," *Chicago Daily Tribune*, July 31, 1954, 17.
12. Richard DeCordova, *Picture Personalities: The Emergence of the Star System in America* (Urbana: University of Illinois Press, 2001), 20.
13. Aljean Harmetz, "Martin Ritt Focuses on Labor Strife," *New York Times*, February 25, 1979, D19.
14. Ibid., D19.

WORKS CITED

Allen, Robert C., and Douglas Gomery. *Film History: Theory and Practice*. Boston: McGraw-Hill, 1985.
Cagle, Chris. *Sociology on Film: Postwar Hollywood's Prestige Commodity*. New Brunswick, NJ: Rutgers University Press, 2017.
DeCordova, Richard. *Picture Personalities: The Emergence of the Star System in America*. Urbana: University of Illinois Press, 2001.
Navasky, Victor S. *Naming Names*. New York: Penguin, 1982.
Neale, Steve. *Genre and Hollywood*. London: Routledge-Taylor and Francis, 2005.
Rogin, Michael. *Blackface, White Noise: Jewish Immigrants in the Hollywood Melting Pot*. Berkeley: University of California Press, 1996.
Ross, Steven J. *Working-Class Hollywood: Silent Film and the Shaping of Class in America*. Princeton, NJ: Princeton University Press, 1998.

Chapter Four

Women, Sex, and Family Conflict on Film

Films about women, gender, romance, and family relations have long been a staple of American movies. Women made up a significant proportion of the movie audience and were assumed to constitute the majority of filmgoers in the 1920s through the 1940s. The US motion picture industry sought to cater to them. Happily-ever-after stories about intrepid heroines, heterosexual love and romance, and dedicated mothers brought female filmgoers into the theaters. But so too did "women's weepies," melodramatic movies about wronged women, romantic and marital relationships gone bad, and long-suffering, sacrificing mothers. Whether comedies or tragedies, movies that directly addressed a female audience and put women characters at the center of the action have come to be considered a genre called "the woman's film." The dramatic and tragic woman's film overlapped with the social problem film, providing another example of the latter genre's hybridity. Social problem films featuring women focused on conflicts related to gender expectations and family relations. These conflicts tended not to be just interpersonal in nature, as in the woman's film, but also to have a public dimension.

In these films, women protagonists faced problems originating at the intersection of private and public life. As discussed in chapter 2, the definitions of *public* and *private* change over time and shape how social problem films approach their subjects and ascertain causes and solutions. Even as these films located the causes of women's problems in both public and private developments, the solutions varied. The political ideology of filmmakers and the popular sociology of the time contributed to these plots. But it is the status of women's reform and feminist movements that had the most profound impact. In historical periods when feminism is flourishing, collective, political action is presented as a way to solve the problems and conflicts women face in their personal lives and relationships. This standpoint was captured in the slogan of the feminist movement of the 1960s and 1970s: "The personal is political." Social problem films with women protagonists from two broad historical periods—the 1910s to the 1930s and the 1980s to the 21st century—provide productive ways to explore the interrelationships among the film genre, the issues and conditions of women's lives at the time, and the impact of feminist activism on American society.

FROM "WHITE SLAVERY" TO "FALLEN WOMAN" FILMS, 1910s–1930s

Social problem films featuring women and focused on prostitution, including a cycle of "white slavery" films and one of "fallen woman" films, had great impact and influence during the Progressive Era to the Great Depression. These films appeared against a backdrop of major changes in women's lives. As the Victorian period of the 19th century transitioned to modern America in the 20th century, the social expectation that women would wholly dedicate themselves to a private life of home and family was on the wane. Although it was never that all American women could adhere to this dominant gender ideology—"the cult of domesticity"—more and more women began to depart from it in the new century. The middle-class "New Woman" and the often-immigrant "working girl" were part of a younger generation engaged in public life through education, wage earning, and Progressive reform movements. They also took up the practice of "going out" to enjoy the new, heterosocial popular amusements available, including the cinema. In the process, they experimented with new sexual behaviors rather than maintaining Victorian manners and morals. Gender and family relations began to alter as women sought more equal companionate marriages and more equal political citizenship. The so-called first wave of feminism in the United States achieved the latter with national women's suffrage in 1920. These developments toward more equal gender relations in private and public life did not occur without social conflict, however.

Such social conflict about women's role and status in society is evident from studying the content and criticism of contemporary social problem films, such as *Traffic in Souls* (1913). *Traffic in Souls* addressed "the social evil" of involuntary prostitution or "white slavery," whereby young women were entrapped and forced into a life of sex work. The term *white slavery* emerged during the Progressive Era as reformers sought to eradicate all forms of prostitution from American life. By targeting and naming white slavery—a heightened and racialized expression—reformers created a moral panic around prostitution. On the national level, they succeeded in securing the 1910 White-Slave Traffic Act, or Mann Act, which prohibited transporting women across state lines for immoral or sexual purposes. On the local level, they achieved the abolition of red-light districts in many cities and states. *Traffic in Souls* was only one of many white slavery films of the silent era, but it was notable, according to scholar Kay Sloan, for striking "the right balance between an educational message and a titillating plot."[1] The first film produced for Universal, *Traffic in Souls* represented a collaboration between filmmakers George Loane Tucker, who directed and developed the story, and Walter MacNamara, who wrote the screenplay and produced. In "filming the story," they were credited at the time with giving "much thought to matters of ethics and policy."[2]

The film's sensational subject required as much. The plot centered on a white slavery syndicate in New York uncovered by Mary Barton, played by Jane Gail, and her fiancé, Officer Burke, played by Matt Moore. They become involved when Mary's sister, Lorna, played by Ethel Grandin, is ensnared by a handsome cad, who drugs her drink during dinner and takes her to a brothel. Multiple story lines intertwine, including when two Swedish immigrant women and a country girl arriving to the city are lured away to a brothel. Jack Cohn's editing involved a new technique at the time: crosscutting between such simultaneous action to juxtapose key events and build suspense. The dramatic rescue of the four women meant they did not, in the end, become "fallen women." In keeping with the genre, *Traffic in Souls* was filmed in a realist style that contemporary reviewers called "photographic." Scenes were shot on Ellis Island, the Upper West Side, and at Penn Station. The filmmakers also made claims of realism and relevance for their story. They promoted their movie as based not on the "vice" novels or plays popular at the time but on the report of a recent legal investigation into forced prostitution in New York City headed by John D. Rockefeller Jr. Rockefeller quickly repudiated the movie, regarding "this method of exploiting vice as not only injudicious, but positively harmful."[3]

Rockefeller's criticism of *Traffic in Souls* presaged the controversy and censorship to come. The film was banned in various localities from Brooklyn to Chicago, Washington, DC, to New Orleans. Some theater owners independently decided not to exhibit the film after receiving negative comments from the moviegoing public. "The picture is immoral and would have a bad effect on the young people," argued a Chicago spokeswoman. The *Moving Picture World*, an industry trade journal, agreed, calling the film "sensational."[4] "There is a time and a place for the discussion of sex problems and that time and place is not in the motion picture theater."[5] In Washington, DC, the Christian Endeavor Union endorsed the banning. They opposed the film as "objectionable," and no doubt some Progressive reformers took issue with the fact that the film's devious head of the white slavery syndicate uses the "International Purity and Reform League" as a front, hinting at hypocrisy among reformers.[6] Many other reformers endorsed *Traffic in Souls*, however.

One, Mrs. S. M. Haggen, president of the Immigrant Girls Home in New York City, reportedly shaped the film project from the start and later screened the film as a warning to newly arrived immigrant women.[7]

Overall, the film was a tremendous success. It was a "prestige picture," six reels or about two hours long (when most films were one or two reels), exhibited in upscale, theatrical venues, and expensive at the ticket booth; filmgoers lined up to see it. *Traffic in Souls* had achieved "the traffic in theatregoers," commented one reviewer.[8] News stories appeared about audiences buzzing with excitement and applauding enthusiastically. Alongside the film's entertainment value, its educational value was lauded. "It is a powerful dramatic full blooded sermon," exclaimed a Connecticut newspaper.[9] The filmmakers' use of many of the conventions of the social problem film were well received. Commentators agreed white slavery was a problem. "Like a pestilent plague, it infects the entire land," analogized the *Atlanta Constitution*.[10] The film's urgent mode of address had an impact. "The story, startling as it is in its truth, has brought the modern New Yorker suddenly to his feet as he realizes the true conditions that exist around him."[11] Spectators also felt empathy for the victimized "fifty thousand girls who disappear every year," as one title in the film states. And the movie's didacticism definitely found an audience. "The scenes . . . show the pitfalls that are laid for young girls in shops, at the large steamship piers, and at the dance halls by the agents of the vice interests."[12] "The picture is a warning to young girls who leave home to find work in the large cities."[13]

What these last two comments reveal is how a film like *Traffic in Souls* and its supporters could work against many of the gains made by women in public life and illuminates the paradox, or mix of progress and reaction, of Progressivism. The movie's message stressed women's vulnerability as they participated in wage work and urban life and discouraged women from venturing outside the family home. Reformer and suffragist Jane Addams wrote on the sexual dangers posed to young women living and working far from "the direct stimulus of family interest or affection."[14] Movie theaters themselves were targeted as "recruiting stations for vice," in the famous words of women's suffrage leader Dr. Anna Howard Shaw.[15] Even as these Progressive reformers campaigned for new rights for women as agents in the public sphere, they equated women's participation in public life with sexual victimization. Rather than seeing *Traffic in Souls* as providing useful instruction, some reformers demanded prohibitions on young people and women seeing white slavery films. They "do nothing more than stimulate an unwholesome and morbid curiosity instead of driving home a moral message," argued one reformer.[16] These films fueled calls for greater movie censorship—a Progressive reform—which culminated in the *Mutual Film Corporation v. Ohio Industrial Commission* (1915) decision.

Another paradoxical outcome of Progressive reform—the outlawing of prostitution—began to shift the definition of the social problem from prostitution to the prostitute herself, and this shift was reflected in later movies. *Traffic in Souls* put the blame squarely on the evil "slavers" who procured women for prostitution. Indirectly indicted are the economic need that forced vulnerable wage-earning women into supplying "the sex trade" and the male debauchery that provided the demand. These causes of prostitution lay in the public sphere. They reflected sociological ideas in circulation at the time about the negative social impact of poverty and the urban environment. And they demanded policing or political solutions. Yet as historian Ruth Rosen argues, the Progressive Era discourse around white slavery and prostitution exonerated "innocent" women, not "immoral" women, of responsibility.[17] Over time, the "degenerate" prostitute came to be defined as the social problem; her condition caused by her personal disgrace and degradation rather than social conditions.

In Hollywood, this change appeared in "fallen woman" films, which were especially popular and featured the greatest female stars in the late 1920s and 1930s, during the era of the Great Depression. These films told stories of unmarried women who lost their chastity or married women who committed adultery, and thus they had "fallen from grace." They are often cast out by their families, suffer social humiliation, and end up as prostitutes, ill, or even dead. In some fallen woman films, the downfall of the main character is due to social factors, such as her or her family's economic need or her limited employment options. In *Blonde Venus* (1932), for example, Marlene Dietrich stars as a married woman and a mother who engages in extramarital sex to pay for her gravely ill husband's medical treatment. But in many other films, the protagonist is a "gold digger" or "kept woman" who chooses this path and uses sex to manipulate men into economically supporting her. In *The Easiest Way* (1931), Constance Bennett's character chooses "the easiest way" of supporting herself: becoming the mistress to a rich man. These two movies happen to have ambiguous endings, presenting the possibility of a solution with the women's return to true love. In most of these films, however, and in the absence of a social or feminist critique, the fallen woman is punished for her transgressions. These motion pictures were very controversial and, along with gangster films, spurred greater enforcement of Hollywood's Production Code in 1934.[18]

Teaching Ideas

These films are useful teaching tools for illuminating the changing conditions and characterizations of American women in the early 20th century. To bring out many of the findings noted above, several strategies are effective.

- The movies mentioned are available as DVDs or online and can be screened in their entirety or in clips.
- To discover the public discussion around these films, examine contemporary newspaper reviews, including the reviews cited. Most of the cited reviews require a subscription with ProQuest Historical Newspapers, but the Google News Archive is freely available. It does not include all newspapers, but it is invaluable for accessing the viewpoints of Americans in smaller towns and cities (https://news.google.com/newspapers). Contemporary books also reveal the larger discourse around and impact of these films. For *Traffic in Souls*, for example, Jane Addams's writings are available online, as is the novelization of the film, one of the first ever in US motion picture history.[19]
- Movie posters can be the focus of small group activities exploring how filmmakers promote their films through advertising and publicity. These elements of a promotional campaign—what media scholars call *paratexts*—aimed to build anticipation and get audiences into theaters. They also established expectations and framed the story for filmgoers. In this way, film promotion both "sells and tells" the movie's narrative.[20] Movie posters, like the one for *Traffic in Souls*, are available online, and students can interpret the meaning of both the images and the text. How is this poster "selling and telling" the story in the movie?

Finally, these movies provide a great opportunity to discuss with students the historical experience of spectatorship for average filmgoers, especially women. Getting at the perspectives of historical filmgoers is challenging due to a lack of primary sources. We can find views and voices of filmmakers, industry representatives, film reviewers, and public commentators. But how can we hear the views and voices of the majority of the audience? Newspaper reviews and reports do indicate the popularity of films, as do box office returns. Sometimes comments appear in print about the enthusiasm and applause of the crowd. Yet often we are left with the challenge of imaginative interpretation. Despite the controversies over white slavery and fallen woman films, women flocked to these movies. Why did they attend, and what did they find there? By reflecting on their own moviegoing, students can imagine some reasons. Scholar Shelley Stamp has provocatively but persuasively argued that women, just as feared by some commentators, found sexual titillation at the white slavery films. But they also gained knowledge about illicit, underground aspects of modern American life and "a form of command over the urban terrain available only at the cinema."[21] It is good to remember as well that the female characters in these films are smart, take action, and often act bravely. Mary Barton in *Traffic in Souls* is a true heroine, a combined representation of the "New Woman" and the "working girl."

Figure 4.1.   © Photofest

Female spectators during the silent era and after undoubtedly enjoyed adventurous women onscreen.[22]

PICTURING WOMEN AND SEXUAL MATTERS AT HOME AND WORK, 1980s–21st CENTURY

The first wave of feminism achieved equal political citizenship for women with the right to vote and numerous other reforms to benefit women and children, including fairer divorce laws and outlawing child labor. But many gender inequalities still existed in public and private life, which the second wave of feminism began to address in the 1960s and 1970s. This generation of women demanded equal pay and credit, equal economic opportunities, and equal access to education. They also defined, named, and sought legislation to deal with crimes such as date and marital rape, domestic violence, and workplace sexual harassment. Like their feminist foremothers in the era of the Progressive reform movements, second-wave feminists were part of a "kaleidoscope of movements."[23] They joined with the civil rights movement, the American Indian and Chicano movements, and the gay liberation and environmental movements, as well as others. Together, these activists propelled social and cultural change and personal and political transformation in the United States. By the 1980s, however, just as many of the gains of the second wave of feminism seemed secure, a conservative backlash ensued. As writer Susan Faludi demonstrated, these opponents of feminism—male, female, individual, and institutional—aimed to roll back women's gains. Hollywood played a role in this backlash with a series of antifeminist films in the 1980s.[24]

Yet more complex pictures of women's private and public lives also appeared in a range of the era's social problem films, such as *Silkwood* (1983). The movie was based on the real-life story of Karen Silkwood, a 28-year-old worker and union activist at a Kerr-McGee Nuclear Corporation Cimarron Plutonium Recycling Facility in Crescent, Oklahoma. Kerr-McGee supplied processed plutonium for the US nuclear power industry. Working with national officials at her Oil, Chemical and Atomic Workers Union (OCAW), Silkwood secretly documented health and safety violations and possible fraud at the facility and then openly testified before the Atomic Energy Commission. In November 1974, she died in a car crash deemed accidental by some but intentional by others. Following her death, a group of activists from a kaleidoscope of movements—the women's, environmental, antinuclear, and civil liberties movements—formed the Karen Silkwood Fund. They joined a successful lawsuit by her estate against Kerr-McGee for violations of nuclear-safety standards. The *New York Times* reported that there were 574 exposures of workers to plutonium at the Cimarron facility between 1970 and 1975, when it closed; it was "a hellish place to work."[25] Director Mike Nichols became interested in making the film due to "the many disquieting circumstances surrounding Karen Silkwood's death." But it "was the manner of her life that marked her out, for history as well as for journalism."[26]

In telling this story, the film simultaneously explored three social problems: the status of women in male-dominated workplaces, corporate exploitation of vulnerable workers, and the dangers of nuclear power. *Silkwood* was also a biopic (a biographical picture) and a political thriller (given the constant fear that Silkwood's undercover research would be discovered), demonstrating again the hybridity of the social problem film genre. The film's realism was evident in the settings and props. The characters inhabit dilapidated houses and drive battered cars. The workplace mise-en-scène evoked the distancing and dangerous nature of the work, even as the workers banter and chew bubblegum. We see Karen Silkwood change into "her laboratory white jumpsuit, getting ready to stick her bare hands inside huge, thick rubber gloves that allow her to touch the lethal plutonium she must work with." Reviewers considered that scene "naturalistic" even if, overall, the film "heightened reality."[27] A harrowing scene when Silkwood is harshly scrubbed down after being contaminated with plutonium and the final shot of her gravestone also exemplified realism. Not all commentators were convinced, however. Supporters of Kerr-McGee lambasted the film as inaccurate and misleading. "What are we to make of 'message' films like *Silkwood*, which grab attention by purporting to be factual [but are not?]"[28] The *New York Times* editorialized that a "docudrama of this type is a meretricious creation" with its "implied authenticity."[29]

This editorial sparked a debate in the newspaper's Letters to the Editor section about *Silkwood*'s various messages and meanings. Some letters came from interested parties, such as director Nichols. Another letter came from a participant in the lawsuit, Jesuit priest William Davis, who argued that the movie was a "substantially accurate dramatization" and could have been even more damning of Kerr-McGee given the facts of the case.[30] One letter stressed how the film raised "serious issues well beyond those of safety in the nuclear industry, including questions about the labor movement [and] feminism."[31] Joining in on these matters was a reader of the *Washington Post* who considered the movie's warning about plutonium, "the most poisonous substance in the universe," much needed.[32] Like this filmgoer, most respondents appreciated *Silkwood*'s didacticism. They agreed that responsibility lay with Kerr-McGee for the social problems depicted in the film. Corporate misdoings—lax manufacturing standards, sloppy health and safety procedures, poor treatment of employees, and anti-unionism—endangered American society. Moreover, these problems required public solutions. Action from the US government's Atomic Energy Commission was required to ensure nuclear safety and to secure labor rights for powerless workers. This liberal message in support of government intervention for the public good mattered very much in the early 1980s. It came just after a conservative Republican president, Ronald Reagan, began to reverse the economic regulations and protections achieved with the New Deal in the 1930s. *Silkwood*'s filmmakers sought to stem this reversal.

The liberal political ideology evident in *Silkwood* dovetailed with the prominence of women both behind the scenes and in front of the camera. The movie starred Meryl Streep as Silkwood and Cher as her best friend, Dolly Pelliker, and the screenwriters were Nora Ephron and Alice Arlen. It was Ephron's first screenplay, and although she later became known for romantic comedies, her movies always had female protagonists. Karen Silkwood's characterization in the film is strong but contradictory. She stands up and takes risks for what is right, but she is not perfectly noble or pure. She is divorced and lives apart from her children in a house with her male lover and Dolly, who is a lesbian. Silkwood drinks, takes drugs, and is less than diligent at work. "She was not a nuclear Joan of Arc, but an activist outraged by terrible working conditions."[33] Film critic Gene Siskel attributed "the richness of her character" to Ephron and Arlen. "Male writers probably would have been tempted to portray Karen as a victim and not much else."[34]

This multifaceted portrayal was mostly—but not wholly—well received by women reviewers. It had "integrity," and spectators "come away admiring Karen Silkwood," contended one reviewer.[35] But Angela Bonavoglia issued a feminist indictment of this characterization in *Cinéaste*. "What gets utterly lost in all this, however, is the development of Karen's social and political commitment, her belief in what she was doing and her willingness to risk anything, including her health and safety, for it." Her longtime union activism and her participation recently in "an abysmally failed strike" are played down in *Silkwood*. When Ephron described Silkwood as "an extremely complicated, occasionally self-destructive woman who was, incidentally, a hero," Bonavoglia exclaimed, "*Incidentally?*" The same would not be said of a man in the same position. "Heroism unrelated to traditional roles eludes women" still, she argued.[36] Marcia Pally pointed out how the depiction of Silkwood—even if accurate—undermined sympathy for her and her cause and constituted "undercover sexism." "Family dirt, homosexuality—in fact, sex of any kind—are juicer stuff than nuclear contamination," she wrote in *Film Comment*. This material distracted audiences from the message of the film, especially as "mainstream audiences generally don't take well to mothers abandoning their children and running around."[37]

That women reviewers could disagree over *Silkwood*'s depiction of a female character written by women indicated the opportunities provided by feminism's newfound place in American society; but as the 1980s and 1990s continued, conservative antifeminism grew. A series of backlash films, led by *Fatal Attraction* (1987), featured single women so crazed by their need for a husband and children that they commit violent and murderous acts. The problem in their lives is their dedication to their careers, which is blamed on feminism, and the solution is a return to traditional women's roles and conservative family values. Despite bad reviews, *Fatal Attraction* was the second-highest-grossing film in 1987 and was nominated for a Best Picture Oscar. That Oscar was won two decades later by *American Beauty* (1999), a film that defined materialistic consumer culture—and the corporate values and class envy behind it—as a social problem. Created by the political and economic changes begun in the 1980s, this culture resulted in family and social dysfunction in the movie. Yet this ostensible critique laid the blame on the wife and mother.[38] Carolyn Burnham, played by Annette Benning, is called "a bloodless, money-grubbing freak" by her husband, Lester, played by Kevin Spacey. Even *Thelma and Louise* (1991), a critique of such antifeminism and misogyny written by a woman, Callie Khouri, ends in the double suicide of the female protagonists rather than in a public solution to the gender inequalities and male violence in their lives.

The rise of a third wave of feminism in the 21st century shaped later social problem films featuring women, including *North Country* (2005) about workplace sexual harassment. *North Country* was "inspired by" real people and events—specifically Lois Jenson and her landmark lawsuit, the first class-action sexual harassment lawsuit in the United States—rather than "based on" real people and events, as was *Silkwood*. This difference meant the filmmakers took more dramatic license with the characters and plot, altering names, events, and even chronology. Directed by Niki Caro from a screenplay by Michael Seitzman, the film starred Charlize Theron as Josey Aimes. When she goes to work in the Minnesota iron mines, a heavily male-dominated workplace, she is subjected to insulting and threatening treatment by her male coworkers. When she seeks support to complain about and change these conditions, she is socially ostracized at home, at work, and in the community. When she decides to sue, her sexual reputation is attacked by her employer. *North Country* has a happy ending, however. The judge allows the case to advance as a class action rather than as an individual lawsuit; the mine agrees to settle, pay damages, and institute a policy prohibiting sexual harassment; and Aimes's reputation is rehabilitated.

The movie's scenario does not convey the full story of Lois Jenson's life or lawsuit. She spent eighteen years working under awful conditions in the mines, from 1975 to 1992, and her lawsuit took fifteen years to resolve, from 1984 to 1998. Despite the early victory of having the case certified as a class action, the legal battle was long, drawn out, and difficult. Jenson suffered emotionally and physically. But with the assumption that audiences would not want to see too much realism, the movie simplified and even suppressed the real events. It did the same with the characterization of Josey Aimes. She is a sympathetic single mother, victimized by rape and abused by her estranged husband. She is not a feminist but needs to work and earn a living to support her children. Lois Jenson's more complicated life, with two children by two different men, including her rapist, and a daughter given up for adoption, was considered too unsympathetic for audiences in the 21st century. This portrayal constituted a change from the complex portrayal of Karen Silkwood two decades earlier. Indeed, one scholar argues that the character of Josey Aimes as a dedicated, self-sacrificing mother fits the genre of the woman's film as much as any other genre, including the social problem film.[39]

But as a social problem film *North Country* did convey the problem of sexual harassment in the workplace, as well as that of domestic violence and rape. It showed these problems as caused by men, allowed to continue by employers, and experienced by women, with devastating effects. The film demonstrated the need for public and, in this case, legal and collective solutions. The film portrayed how fighting back through the legal system puts an individual woman's reputation, physical health, and mental well-being at risk. By joining together, women can have power and safety in numbers. At least this part of *North Country*'s happy ending matched reality and showed how important a class-action approach to sexual harassment can be.

Teaching Ideas

As with the films discussed in the first section, the films in this section are useful teaching tools for illuminating the conditions and characterizations of women in the late 20th and early 21st centuries. The strategies discussed above are still useful to reveal how and why these movies were produced and consumed: screening movies and clips; examining contemporary news coverage, reviews, books, and movie posters; and encouraging students to consider the range of possibilities for reception.

For these more recent films, box office returns and Academy Awards can reveal a film's popularity with average filmgoers and its regard within the Hollywood motion picture industry. This information is available on the major movie website IMDb (www.imdb.com/). The website Rotten Tomatoes provides comments from both critics and filmgoers (www.rottentomatoes.com/). A good discussion to have with students is to consider who comments on such websites. Understanding that these commenters are a self-selected, motivated portion of the movie audience may limit the representativeness of their opinions. But we still can use their reactions, compliments, and criticisms to gauge how effectively filmmakers conveyed the message and meaning of their films.

An interesting development in the social problem film genre to consider is how over time more and more of these films tell the story of real people and events, whether "based on" or "inspired by" actual history. Given the generic convention of realism for the social problem film, growing audience sophistication and demand for verisimilitude perhaps required this change.

What this development allows for is a useful compare-and-contrast analysis of the representation and interpretation of social problems in a dramatic film and what can be found in other sources, including in print and documentaries. For example, books on Karen Silkwood and Lois Jenson exist, as do video documentaries.

- Richard Rashke, *The Killing of Karen Silkwood: The Story Behind the Kerr-McGee Plutonium Case*, 2nd ed. (Ithaca, NY: Cornell University Press, 2000).
- *A Life on the Line—Karen Silkwood Documentary*, A&E documentary,www.youtube.com/watch?v=J2BoqzeJAV4.
- Clara Bingham and Laura Leedy Gansler, *Class Action: The Landmark Case That Changed Sexual Harassment Law* (New York: Anchor Books, 2002).
- *Class Action*, C-Span documentary of Bingham and Gansler discussion of their book,www.c-span.org/video/?171728-1/class-action.

Asking students how these representations and interpretations differ and to hypothesize about why they differ can lead to fruitful discussions. Were the facts too difficult or challenging for popular audiences? How did filmmakers use their dramatic license and to what effect? Do these departures from fact hurt or help the message they are trying to get across?

Historian Robert Rosenstone argues that all historical films must simplify and compress the story they are telling about the past. Not every fact known about the past can be included, otherwise it would overload the story. At times, filmmakers also invent characters and events to move their story along. Rosenstone says these inventions can be true or false. Although a "true invention" sounds like a contradiction in terms, he contends true inventions fit with what we know about what really happened. They did not happen, but they could have happened; it is possible. "False inventions" are completely counterfactual and violate "the discourse of history," as he puts it.[40]

Both kinds of inventions need to be acknowledged and analyzed, but do we agree that true inventions are acceptable and false inventions are not? Are we comfortable with such slippage between fact and fiction, or do we advocate a hard line? What are the consequences of filmmakers adhering to a hard line? Would anyone come to see their movies? Is it better to expose audiences to these stories about social problems, even if not every aspect is true? Or does that damage the credibility of filmmakers and the legitimacy of social problem films? All good food for thought in our classrooms.

NOTES

1. Kay Sloan, *The Loud Silents: Origins of the Social Problem Film* (Urbana: University of Illinois Press, 1998), 82.
2. George Blaisdell, "Traffic in Souls," *Moving Picture World*, November 22, 1913, 849.
3. John D. Rockefeller Jr., quoted in Frank P. Morse, "The Traffic in Theatergoers," *Washington Post*, December 21, 1913, MT2.
4. "Bars Out 'Traffic in Souls,'" *Chicago Daily Tribune*, January 1, 1914, 23.
5. Epes Winthrop Sargent, "Advertising for Exhibitors," *Moving Picture World*, February 28, 1914, 1079.
6. "'Slave' Films Shown," *Washington Post*, December 23, 1913, 2.
7. Lee Grieveson, "Policing the Cinema: *Traffic in Souls* at Ellis Island, 1913," *Screen* 38 (Summer 1997): 149–71.
8. Morse, "Traffic in Theatergoers," MT2.
9. "'Traffic in Souls' at the Life Today," *Meriden Morning Record*, October 18, 1915, https://news.google.com/newspapers?id=-GE1AAAAIBAJ&sjid=GxQLAAAAIBAJ&pg=2641%2C1331705.
10. "Excellent Entertainment at Local Theaters This Week," *Atlanta Constitution*, January 18, 1914, B6.
11. "Amusements," *Lewiston Daily Sun*, March 21, 1914, https://news.google.com/newspapers?id=prUgAAAAIBAJ&sjid=fWkFAAAAIBAJ&pg=4908%2C4689549.
12. "Vice Film at Weber's," *New York Times*, November 23, 1913, X6.
13. "Traffic in Souls," *Kentucky New Era*, May 19, 1914, https://news.google.com/newspapers?id=doIhAAAAIBAJ&sjid=64sFAAAAIBAJ&pg=4760%2C4296770.
14. Jane Addams, quoted in Shelley Stamp, *Movie Struck Girls: Women and Motion Picture Culture after the Nickelodeon* (Princeton, NJ: Princeton University Press, 2000), 72.
15. Anna Howard Shaw, quoted in Stamp, *Movie Struck Girls*, 47.
16. Stephen S. Wise, quoted in Stamp, *Movie Struck Girls*, 67.
17. Ruth Rosen, *The Lost Sisterhood: Prostitution in America, 1900–1918* (Baltimore: Johns Hopkins University Press, 1982), 48.
18. Lea Jacobs, *The Wages of Sin: Censorship and the Fallen Woman Film, 1928–1942* (Madison: University of Wisconsin Press, 1991).
19. Jane Addams, "Amelioration of Economic Conditions," *A New Conscience and an Ancient Evil* (New York: MacMillan, 1912): 55–94, http://hullhouse.uic.edu/hull/urbanexp/main.cgi?file=new/show_doc.ptt&doc=796&chap=43; Eustace Hale Ball, *Traffic in Souls: A Novel of Crime and Its Cure*, https://books.google.co.nz/books?id=YmXyQJJO910C&printsec=frontcover&source=gbs_ge_summary_r&cad=0#v=onepage&q&f=false.
20. Lisa Kernan, *Coming Attractions: Reading American Movie Trailers* (Austin: University of Texas Press, 2004); Jonathan Gray, *Show Sold Separately: Promos, Spoilers, and Other Media Paratexts* (New York: New York University Press, 2010).
21. Stamp, *Movie Struck Girls*, 98.
22. Nan Enstad, "Dressed for Adventure: Working Women and Silent Movie Serials in the 1910s," *Feminist Studies* 21, no. 1 (1995): 67–90.
23. This phrase inspired by Terry H. Anderson, *The Movement and the Sixties* (New York: Oxford University Press, 1995), preface.
24. Susan Faludi, *Backlash: The Undeclared War against American Women* (New York: Anchor Books, 1991).
25. William J. Broad, "Fact and Legend Clash in 'Silkwood,'" *New York Times*, December 11, 1983, H23.
26. Mike Nichols, "On Telling the Real Karen Silkwood's Story," *New York Times*, January 8, 1984, E24.
27. Gene Siskel, "'Silkwood': Beyond the Conspiracies, a Film That Works," *Chicago Tribune*, December 14, 1983, E1
28. Nick Thimmesch, "'Silkwood': Martyrdom or Fantasy?" *Washington Post*, December 11, 1983, L1. See also Nick Thimmesch, "Silkwood: Fact, Fiction," *Herald-Journal*, December 19, 1983, https://news.google.com/newspapers?id=FVcsAAAAIBAJ&sjid=w84EAAAAIBA

J&pg=5202%2C6123654.

29. "The Chicanery of 'Silkwood,'" *New York Times*, December 25, 1983, E12.

30. William Davis, "A 'Substantially Accurate' Drama about Karen Silkwood," *New York Times*, January 11, 1984, A22.

31. Victor A. Kovner, "What 'Silkwood' Is—and Is Not," *New York Times*, January 7, 1984, 22.

32. A. L. Hengst, "'Silkwood': The Real Hazard," *Washington Post*, January 13, 1984, A22.

33. Broad, "Fact and Legend Clash," H23.

34. Siskel, "'Silkwood,'" E1.

35. Marsha Fottler, "Streep Excels Again in Gutsy 'Silkwood,'" *Sarasota Herald-Tribune*, January 13, 1984, https://news.google.com/newspapers?id=QW4fAAAAIBAJ&sjid=mGgEAAAAIBAJ&pg=5932%2C2355644.

36. Angela Bonavoglia, review of *Silkwood*, directed by Mike Nicholas, *Cinéaste* 13, no. 3 (1984): 39–40.

37. Marcia Pally, "Fool's Gold," *Film Comment* 20 (May–June 1984): 31.

38. Kathleen Rowe Karlyn, "'Too Close for Comfort': *American Beauty* and the Incest Motif," *Cinema Journal* 44 (Fall 2004): 82.

39. Orit Kamir, "*North Country*'s Hero and Her Cinematic Lawyer: Can 'Lawyer Films' and 'Women's Films' Merge to Launch a New Feminist Sub-genre?" *Canadian Journal of Women and the Law* 21, no. 1 (2009): 129–33.

40. Robert A. Rosenstone, *Visions of the Past: The Challenge of Film to Our Idea of History* (Cambridge, MA: Harvard University Press, 1995), 72–73.

WORKS CITED

Anderson, Terry H. *The Movement and the Sixties*. New York: Oxford University Press, 1995.

Bonavoglia, Angela. Review of *Silkwood*, directed by Mike Nichols. *Cinéaste* 13, no. 3 (1984): 38–40.

Enstad, Nan. "Dressed for Adventure: Working Women and Silent Movie Serials in the 1910s." *Feminist Studies* 21, no. 1 (1995): 67–90.

Faludi, Susan. *Backlash: The Undeclared War against American Women*. New York: Anchor Books, 1991.

Gray, Jonathan. *Show Sold Separately: Promos, Spoilers, and Other Media Paratexts*. New York: New York University Press, 2010.

Grieveson, Lee. "Policing the Cinema: *Traffic in Souls* at Ellis Island, 1913." *Screen* 38 (Summer 1997): 149–71.

Jacobs, Lea. *The Wages of Sin: Censorship and the Fallen Woman Film, 1928–1942*. Madison: University of Wisconsin Press, 1991.

Kamir, Orit. "*North Country*'s Hero and Her Cinematic Lawyer: Can 'Lawyer Films' and 'Women's Films' Merge to Launch a New Feminist Sub-genre?" *Canadian Journal of Women and the Law* 21, no. 1 (2009): 119–42.

Karlyn, Kathleen Rowe. "'Too Close for Comfort': *American Beauty* and the Incest Motif." *Cinema Journal* 44 (Fall 2004): 69–93.

Kernan, Lisa. *Coming Attractions: Reading American Movie Trailers*. Austin: University of Texas Press, 2004.

Neale, Steve. *Genre and Hollywood*. London and New York: Routledge, 2000.

Pally, Marcia. "Fool's Gold." *Film Comment* 20 (May–June 1984): 28–32.

Roffman, Peter, and Jim Purdy. *The Hollywood Social Problem Film: Madness, Despair and Politics from the Depression to the Fifties*. Bloomington: Indiana University Press, 1981.

Rosen, Ruth. *The Lost Sisterhood: Prostitution in America, 1900–1918*. Baltimore: Johns Hopkins University Press, 1982.

Rosenstone, Robert A. *Visions of the Past: The Challenge of Film to Our Idea of History*. Cambridge, MA: Harvard University Press, 1995.

Sloan, Kay. *The Loud Silents: Origins of the Social Problem Film*. Urbana: University of Illinois Press, 1998.

Stamp, Shelley. *Movie Struck Girls: Women and Motion Picture Culture after the Nickelodeon.* Princeton, NJ: Princeton University Press, 2000.

Chapter Five

Projecting Racial and Ethnic Prejudice in the Social Problem Film

The chapter on labor and class conflict noted that the social problem film is never just about one thing. The labor and class conflict social problem film is almost always about labor and class conflict plus something else. *Salt of the Earth* (1954) nominally was based on a real-life strike that took place against the Empire Zinc Company. But the film also could not ignore that the strikers were Mexican Americans who faced injustices and unequal treatment when compared to white miners or the role Mexican American women played during that strike. The chapter also noted that in order to fully understand how the social problem film worked in engaging these issues, we needed to follow a systematic process that could build upon the work of others, identify gaps in knowledge or weaknesses in understanding, develop an overriding idea or premise using other ideas and evidence to support claims, and then make an argument for what has changed as a result of the contribution your thinking and argument has made.

Another aspect of this process involves putting ideas to the test. Indeed, we want to invite others to poke holes in the argument. That skepticism is part of the process. If after being tested the idea still holds, then we know it must be a pretty good idea. If the idea doesn't hold, then perhaps it just needs some revision and refurbishment. And sometimes, very rarely, a reigning idea completely falls apart under the test, and we must come up with a whole new system for how we understand what we examine. Most new ideas regarding film history are not revolutionary in the order of magnitude of completely disproving something, like showing that the earth is not flat or that the sun and stars do not rotate in orbit around us. But even incremental change and increased precision in our understanding can make a contribution to our overall knowledge about the social problem film.

We previously explored how the process works when we applied it to understanding the labor and class conflict social problem film. But how do we know whether the process would work in better understanding other kinds of social problem films? We would want to see if we could apply the same steps to understanding how the social problem film treated the topic of racial and ethnic prejudice. We will set some basic ground rules. We should be able to remove any one of these steps and show that it can be an effective part of a classroom discussion or exercise. And, together and as part of a systematic process, these steps can help lead us to a deeper understanding of how the social problem film works as a genre. In other words, every aspect of this process that we used to trace the development of how the social problem film treated labor and class conflict should work equally well for understanding how the social problem film treated racial and ethnic prejudice.

To put this process to the test, then, we would need to do seven things:

- Identify an academic problem involving one or more social problem films depicting race and ethnic prejudice.
- Explain why that problem should matter to someone other than just you.
- Propose an overriding idea involving the race and ethnic prejudice social problem film that you can develop and test and that in the end will solve something we don't know or that we think we understand but really don't.
- Explain how your work on one or more race and ethnic prejudice social problem films builds upon the work of a community of scholars who already have laid some groundwork for your research to occur.
- Advance your overriding idea with a series of smaller ideas involving the race and ethnic prejudice social problem film, and if you are writing a paper, try to preview each one of the steps you take to develop your overriding idea as early as possible.
- Offer primary evidence related to race and ethnic prejudice social problem films to support your claims.
- Explain for the community of people who care about this subject what has changed or will change as a result of the scholarship you contribute on the race and ethnic prejudice social problem film.

IDENTIFYING AN ACADEMIC PROBLEM FOR THE RACIAL AND ETHNIC PREJUDICE SOCIAL PROBLEM FILM

What would an academic problem for the racial and ethnic prejudice social problem film look like? In "Citizen Chicano," Chon Noriega argued that scholars have not looked closely enough at narratives for ten social problem films, *Salt of the Earth* among them, released between 1935 and 1962. Noriega maintained that rather than look at these films as more generic cultural indicators of Mexican American identities, their narratives revealed explicit manifestations for how to determine and reinforce "the appropriate place for the Mexican American character" as both a US citizen and as an "Other."[1] Noriega identifies a gap in scholarship on depictions of Mexican Americans in these social problem films. Namely, that few scholars were discussing either these films specifically or the ways in which their specific narratives reflected both ambiguous and ambivalent attitudes about Mexican American citizens. Even in a politically progressive film like *Salt of the Earth*, Noriega argued, the film problematically conflated Mexican American identity within a broader array of "labor, racial, and gender issues."[2] That complex asserted assimilation and integration of this identity in ways that Anglo-American audiences, rather than Hispanic ones, might find appealing and compelling.

Noriega's analysis still leaves a gap in our knowledge of the film, and it is a big one. He readily admitted that in-depth analysis of any one of the ten films was beyond the scope of his project. So right there, handed to us on a silver platter, would be a ready-made problem ripe for further analysis. Judging from this article alone, we still do not know if a closer analysis of just *Salt of the Earth* would bear out Noriega's main thesis. We also might want to test another idea Noriega presents. Noriega's article presented no evidence regarding how Mexican American audiences might have responded to a film like *Salt of the Earth*. Noriega used a text-based method to perform close analyses of narrative motifs and patterns tying together his list of ten social problem films depicting Mexican Americans, so he didn't necessarily have to research audience responses to the film as well. But that gap in that article created a new opportunity to conduct further research that could help refine and revise this particular reading of the film.

Noriega's analysis suggested that both teachers and students could learn larger cultural lessons from the specifics of how social problem films self-consciously depicted prejudice. You also should consider the role race and ethnicity played in the development of both the industry and its audience. You should consider the role Hollywood played in purveying racial and ethnic stereotypes and how these stereotypes, while sometimes harmful, frequently worked in complex ways and had different appeals for different audiences. You should consider how Hollywood itself frequently came under attack based on ethnic prejudice. And finally, you should consider how Hollywood often simply omitted race and ethnicity and how that omission was itself a form of prejudice. Like the chapter on labor and class conflict, this chapter looks at how the genre—as a genre—tackled racial and ethnic prejudice. How it tackled this subject may tell us more about the inner workings of how the genre operated than it reveals about how racial and ethnic prejudice actually and materially embedded themselves within the fabric of American life. However, when viewed alongside a historical record and within a broader context, these images might reveal something of the cultural push and pull between various forces vying for control within pluralistic societies.

We should ask why one might care about how social problem films treated racial and ethnic prejudice if what they ultimately offered remained different from the actual lived experience of racial and ethnic prejudice in the United States. One way to address this question of significance would be to consider the cost of not looking closely at this particular group of films. For some, these films offered idealized visions of what American pluralism could be like. The tension between such ideals and reality might tell us something about American cultural identity. For others, the ideals reveal a failure of courage and imagination, one where the mainstream film industry ultimately was unable to take anything other than the most timid of stands or risk the wrath of reactionary forces within American civic society. For still others, the films could reveal a kind of ongoing negotiation between competing liberal and conservative ideologies, all vying for control over what American pluralism might look like.

The chapter cannot definitely resolve these debates. By focusing on how the social problem film depicted prejudice, we are leaving out much material, such as films that just happened to include one character of a particular race or ethnicity. It also overlooks social problem films that problematically relied on racial or ethnic stereotypes, as opposed to the films that self-consciously attempt to address these stereotypes. Rather, this chapter considers how the genre continued to develop a mode of address that explicitly spoke to audiences about racial and ethnic prejudice. We then consider how these films attempted to leverage the topicality of major social and political events, such as the Holocaust or civil rights struggles. Next, the chapter examines how the social problem film treated race and ethnic prejudice in ways that reaffirmed the status quo. Finally, the chapter looks at the flexibility of the genre in depicting race and ethnic prejudice in ways that challenged social orthodoxies.

The overriding premise of this chapter argues that the way in which social problem films treated racial and ethnic prejudice developed a specific mode of address that changed over time to suit different social crises and emergent social groups and their interests. While the chapter won't actually solve the problem of racial and ethnic prejudice in general, it might solve some academic problems, mainly about what we know or don't know about how the social problem film depicted prejudice. For example, in order to understand how the genre developed a way to address audiences regarding racial and ethnic prejudice, we might ask how much we know about some of the earliest American films to tackle this subject as a social problem and as a central concern of the narrative.

Because so much of academic inquiry involves solving problems of knowledge and understanding, we want to review existing literature to identify current gaps and weaknesses in what we know of how social problem films tackled this subject. We know from Noriega's article on Chicanos that examining characters out of context from their narratives is not enough. However, Noriega's analysis focused on representations of Chicano/as. From that article alone, we don't know if subsequent scholarship has used Noriega's approach to look at representations of other ethnic and racial groups in social problem films. Were we to take his approach in looking at other, earlier examples of treating race prejudice, we would want to find more scholarship treating this topic. That search would look for secondary scholarship considering not just characters in social problem films but the place that existed for those characters in those narratives. The combination of the kinds of characters as well as the narratives in which they appeared might, in turn, tell us something about the voice these films used to address audiences regarding racial and ethnic prejudice. Finally, while we may know something about the characters in early race films treating race prejudice, scholarship arguably has paid less attention to how the narratives of these early films of the 1920s shaped Hollywood's later treatment of racial and ethnic prejudice.

A thorough review of scholarly literature would need to develop a research strategy to examine whether relevant books and journal articles already had addressed these questions. We also have a premise that would require further confirmation. I suspect few have chosen to take Noriega's approach in considering how narratives represent ethnic and racial groups. At the same time, the premise is overly broad and difficult to render down into finite search terms. An easier task would be to isolate a particular name or film title and then see if we could find scholarship treating those specific topics. We might even want to break down the question further. What were some of the earliest examples of social problem films tackling ethnic and racial prejudice? From there, we would be able to address at least part of the problem: a gap in our understanding of how early social problem film narratives treated ethnic and racial prejudice. Subsequent work, done either by us or by others, then could use this scholarship to examine how these films may or may not have shaped Hollywood's later treatment of this subject.

Were we to further explore the idea, we could look to some general sources to see what they have to say about these early films and their treatment of ethnic and racial prejudice. These sources may or may not fit the definition of a scholarly resource. Your textbook, for example, is considered a tertiary resource. For a literature review, you typically will want to use secondary resources—in other words, resources that use primary evidence to perform some level of criticism and analysis. Tertiary resources like textbooks, though, can help point you to the right secondary resources. In their textbook *America on Film: Representing Race, Class, Gender, and Sexuality at the Movies*, Harry Benshoff and Sean Griffin argued that early attempts to treat racial prejudice in films emerged from "independently produced black-cast films which were distributed to black movie theaters from the late 1910s to the 1950s." While they noted that compared to Hollywood films, these small independent features were "cheaply made and technically inferior," what these films offered instead were "more complex images of African-Americans and their concerns." The best-known director of this period, African American independent filmmaker Oscar Micheaux, made films offering "a range of black characters, from middle-class professionals to illiterate Southern sharecroppers."[3]

This tertiary source now gives us some valuable perspective on these early films. We have a name, Oscar Micheaux. We know that the films were largely independently produced, outside mainstream Hollywood, and that they flourished between the 1910s and 1950s. Around the 1950s was when Hollywood began producing its own social problem films directly addressing racial and ethnic prejudice. While a more thorough search of secondary scholarship would look for articles that spoke in greater depth about Micheaux, about independent African American filmmaking, about filmmaking during the 1910–1950 time period, this focus helps target our search for knowledge and get back the results we need to move forward.

RACIAL AND ETHNIC PREJUDICE SOCIAL PROBLEM FILMS WITHIN AND OUTSIDE HOLLYWOOD

One Micheaux film in particular, *Within Our Gates* (1920) is a significant film not just in terms of the social problem genre but also in terms of its intertextuality, its pioneering depiction of racism and lynching for the time, and its marking the birth of what many scholars consider to be an authentic African American cinema. One can understand the social problem film as interlocking with other emergent strands within the development of the film industry. While several westerns already had depicted lynchings or the threat of lynchings, *Within Our Gates* was the first African American film to mark the specificity of these acts in targeting African Americans. It also encouraged readings of the film seeing it as a response to Griffith's infamous *Birth of a Nation*. *Birth of a Nation* dealt with race prejudice too, as well as incurring its own charges of perpetuating that prejudice. Yet its glorification of the Ku Klux Klan operated under the socially acceptable guise of historical epic. That film made more sense as a historical blockbuster and part of an ever-popular cycle of Civil War films produced during the 1910s and 1920s that culminated with *Gone with the Wind* (1939).

The director of *Within Our Gates*, Oscar Micheaux, already was an established novelist who frequently adapted his own works for the screen. Micheaux's films, unlike most Hollywood films, frequently included all or mostly African American casts. With the exception of some novelty features, such as religiously inspired allegories like *Green Pastures* or *Hallelujah*, or musicals, such as *Cabin in the Sky* or *Stormy Weather*, mainstream Hollywood would not embrace the all-black, serious, dramatic feature film set in the contemporary United States until *Raisin in the Sun*.

Were we to advance the earlier overriding idea that social problem films treated racial and ethnic prejudice developed a specific but changing mode of address to suit different social crises and emergent social groups and their interests, we might make a smaller claim here. Just as significantly, Hollywood during the 1930s also made social problem films that dealt with lynching but without specifying race or ethnicity. Rather than directly engage anti-Semitism, for example, Mervyn LeRoy's *They Won't Forget* depicted the famous lynching of Leo Frank, a Jewish factory owner in Atlanta. Yet the film never once mentioned either Frank's name or his ethnicity. Instead, the film presented the problem as once between the North and South. Micheaux also dealt with the Leo Frank lynching, first in 1921 with the now lost *Gunsaulus Mystery* (1922) and later in the remake, *Murder in Harlem* (1935).

To support this claim that Hollywood social problem films like *They Won't Forget* did not treat lynching with the same racial and ethnic specificity as independent African American films, we would want to offer primary evidence. With film, that primary evidence could be something as simple as a plot description. As an exercise, using IMDb, for example, find the plot description for Micheaux's *Murder in Harlem* (1935) and LeRoy's *They Won't Forget* (1937). What are the similarities between the plots? What are the differences? What do those differences suggest about how each film treats lynching? Were you to then watch and compare each film, what kind of things would you look for?[4]

Two other Hollywood antilynching films, *Black Legion* (1936) and *Fury* (1936), dealt with lynching but again despecified race and ethnicity. *Black Legion* depicted a man who gets involved with a group very much like the Ku Klux Klan after he's passed over for promotion by someone else named Dombrowski. *Fury* depicted mob rule after a man is wrongly accused of murder. While many hailed the films and the studio that made them, Warner Bros., as courageous, others felt the studio did not go far enough in identifying racial and ethnic hatred as the problem driving lynching.

THE HOLLYWOOD ANTI-SEMITISM AND ANTIRACISM SOCIAL PROBLEM FILM OF THE 1940s AND 1950s

The end of World War II spawned a cycle of social problem films addressing anti-Semitism, including *Crossfire* (1946) and *Gentleman's Agreement* (1947). *Crossfire* was a hybrid film noir–social problem film. It was based on a novel about the cover-up of a murder committed by a military man. In the novel, the victim was gay, but the movie transposed the victim to a Jew. In *Gentleman's Agreement*, the film exposed polite anti-Semitism in America by having a Christian journalist go undercover as a Jew.

Both of these films offer opportunities for discussing how they existed within a larger context. This discussion could easily occur within the context of a classroom by addressing specific questions based on a short clip or movie review from the film's time period. How do you think public awareness of the Holocaust played into the making of these films? What reasons do you think the films had for focusing on anti-Semitism in American life instead of focusing on Nazi anti-Semitism and the ultimate outcome of genocide? A teacher also could build a lesson around comparing and contrasting two short scenes from *Crossfire* and *Gentleman's Agreement*. In what ways do these films operate according to the unwritten rules of the social problem film (e.g., Where is the urgency? Are there social institutions that work to reform the problem?). How do these films operate visually and narratively in very different ways? What is the look (lighting, camerawork, acting style, etc.)? Judging from the clips chosen in advance, what can we say about how the film behaves as a hybrid, between being a social problem film plus something else, such as film noir or a romantic drama?

The late 1940s brought yet another cycle of American antiracism social problems films, and with this cycle, came a particular set of patterns for depicting the problem and the solution. The problem, as manifest in these films, stemmed from "a few bad apples." Racism was an individual neurosis to be cured either by rooting out psychological deviance or by training the African American male to live in a white world. That world, of course, hardly saw itself as white. The solution, then, pointed to institutions—law, medicine, police—that could do the work of mediating between psychotic racism, on one hand, and the culturally illiterate African American male, on the other.

The 1950s social problem film also brought about the rise of the African American superstar Sidney Poitier. Poitier, born to Bahamian parents, became known for choosing dignified roles and became associated with unassailable and perhaps unattainable perfection for African American males. In films such as *No Way Out* or *The Defiant Ones*, he is willing to nobly sacrifice himself for the well-being of the racist white character. In order to better understand these roles in the context of the time, we might treat the star text of Sidney Poitier throughout the 1950s as a form of primary evidence. How did these characters and roles work across multiple films? What do magazines and newspapers have to say about these roles at the time? How does Poitier talk about race in interviews he gave? What does he see those films doing? How does his personal biography play into his choice of roles?

The 1950s also are notable for the absent minority victim. In films such as *Bad Day at Black Rock*, *Trial*, or *Twelve Angry Men*, the victims, either murdered or framed for a murder, remain largely mute within the overall narrative. *Bad Day at Black Rock* is one of the few films of this period to explore anti-Asian racism. Both *Trial* and *12 Angry Men* revolve around racist and exploitative forces swirling around a wrongly accused Hispanic adolescent. Yet in these films, their narratives focus upon white men struggling to ensure justice prevails within a predominantly white system.

THE RACIAL AND ETHNIC PREJUDICE SOCIAL PROBLEM FILM IN THE NEW HOLLYWOOD

The practice of adapting live television dramas and their cross-fertilization with successful social problem films had already begun with *12 Angry Men* and continued into the early 1960s. To view the social problem film as unique to Hollywood ignores the round-robin influence this media had upon the genre. *The Pawnbroker* shared many features with television, including director Sidney Lumet, who came from live television and who went back to working on series television after the film. The filmmakers also tried every major Hollywood studio before releasing *The Pawnbroker* as an independent film. No one wanted to touch it because it dealt directly with a Holocaust survivor. The film also drew upon an urban environment and featured multiple ethnicities.

The race and ethnicity social problem film also relied upon adaptations of already-written novels and plays. Not only did these films already have built-in audiences, but the films could leverage the cultural capital of their source material. And if the films were controversial, the films could have plausible deniability. The plot lines and motifs worked and achieved critical respectability in their highbrow form.

The late 1960s and early 1970s brought about new cultural freedoms. The film industry abandoned its previous system of self-regulation in favor of its current-day rating system. This allowed films like *Guess Who's Coming to Dinner*, *In the Heat of the Night*, and *To Sir, with Love* to treat taboo themes—interracial romance, police racism, racism in education—with a new frankness. Taken to its extremes, *Sweet Sweetback's Badass Song* could use the industry's X rating to point to the extratextual racism that existed and could not tolerate an all-black action-adventure movie in which the outlaw does not pay for his crimes. That film launched a completely different genre, that of the blaxpoitation film.

Did these other genres and media supplant the role of the social problem film and its serious treatment of ethnic and racial prejudice? During the 1970s, blaxpoitation films, sequels (*They Call Me Mr. Tibbs*), comedy (*Blaz-*

ing Saddles), and other genres outside the social problem genre proliferated. A few African American–oriented features struck a more earnest tone but often emphasized family entertainment (*Sounder*), biopics (*Leadbelly*), or featured slice-of-life comedy (*The Landlord* or *Claudine*) and didn't necessarily follow the social problem film's insistence that there was a clear-cut solution to the problems of racism. Further research might look to television, especially the made-for-television movie, as supplanting the role of the social problem film. In addition to television series, notable TV movies like *To All My Friends on Shore*, *The Autobiography of Miss Jane Pittman*, or arguably even miniseries like *Roots: The Next Generations* all fulfilled the role of the modern social problem film in tackling issues of racial and ethnic prejudice.

The cycle of the modern ethnic and racial prejudice social problem film returned with a generation of independent black filmmakers breaking through to the Hollywood mainstream in the 1980s and early 1990s. While many of the issues initially taken up by the conventional Hollywood social problem film ended up in different genres and modalities, films such as *Do the Right Thing*, *Boyz n the Hood*, and *Menace II Society* appeared to return the subject of an African American experience, an experience that frequently included encounters with racism and prejudice at many societal levels, to the center of mainstream Hollywood. Like the rise of the independently financed actor-producer packages that revolutionized Hollywood in the late 1960s and early 1970s, these films demonstrated that Hollywood movies could tackle difficult subjects seriously, unflinchingly, in ways that were socially relevant, and beyond the genres and modalities of action-adventure, comedy, or so-called family films.

The ethnic and racial prejudice social problem film also diversified its races and ethnicities throughout this period. One should be careful to differentiate between films that simply reference or include another race or ethnicity and those that address prejudice within the terms of the social problem film. Independent films such as *El Norte* (1983) depicted the plight of undocumented immigrants. Native Americans, apart from stereotypes in westerns and comedies, had appeared in social problem films since the 1920s. Kent Mackenzie directed the 1961 docudrama *The Exiles*, which depicted the plight of displaced Native Americans. Films such as *Skins* (2002) addressed the social problems of living on the reservation. At the same time, more recent cycles of social problem films have taken up prejudice itself as a social problem, regardless of its ethnic and racial targets. Films such as *American History X* (1998), *House of Sand and Fog* (2003), and *Crash* (2004) all show the extreme consequences of racism and prejudice gone unchecked.

Ultimately, these films should raise questions in your classrooms. How do their depictions differ from our understanding today of racial and ethnic prejudice? In what ways do these films strive to achieve topicality and relevance, and how would an audience at the time they were released understand the narratives and imagery of these films? And finally, how do these films attempt to achieve a level of sincerity and seriousness that is consistent with the social problem film as a genre, as opposed to other genres that might casually address racial and ethnic prejudice within other modalities and frameworks, such as documentary, action-adventure, comedy, and the like?

NOTES

1. Chon Noriega, "Citizen Chicano: The Trials and Titillations of Ethnicity in the American Cinema, 1935–1962," *Social Research* 58, no. 2 (1991): 413–38.
2. Ibid., 424.
3. Harry M. Benshoff and Sean Griffin, *America on Film: Representing Race, Class, Gender, and Sexuality at the Movies*, 2nd ed. (Malden, MA: Blackwell, 2009), 81.
4. A lengthier and more detailed treatment of this comparison appears in Matthew Bernstein, *Screening a Lynching: The Leo Frank Case on Film and Television* (Athens: University of Georgia Press, 2009).

WORKS CITED

Benshoff, Harry M., and Sean Griffin. *America On Film: Representing Race, Class, Gender, and Sexuality at the Movies*. 2nd ed. Malden, MA: Blackwell, 2009.
Bernstein, Matthew. *Screening a Lynching: The Leo Frank Case on Film and Television*. Athens: University of Georgia Press, 2009.
Noriega, Chon. "Citizen Chicano: The Trials and Titillations of Ethnicity in the American Cinema, 1935–1964." *Social Research* 58, no. 2 (1991): 413–38.

Chapter Six

Screening Private Illness and Public Health

Social problem films about physical and mental illness chart a change over time in how they are defined and treated, as well as sufferers' experience of illness and the social consequences. Ideas about what constitutes, causes, and cures illness begin with medical professionals, who aim to influence popular understandings. The US motion picture industry plays a role in this process. Social problem films can help to disseminate the latest medical knowledge about existing or newly discovered diseases and disabilities. They can explore their effects on the individual, families, and communities and the best approaches to treating or managing such disabilities or diseases. In the process, these films can reinforce old ways or present new ways to approach illness. At different historical moments, illness was understood as the personal fault or moral failing of the individual rather than the result of forces beyond their control. The sufferer then was viewed as an agent, rather than a victim, of his or her condition. Social problem films seek to evoke sympathy for the characters onscreen. Yet in some cases, our sympathies may not lie with the sufferer, whom we blame for his or her illness, but with those around the sufferer. Whether a film portrays private, public, or a mix of factors as the cause of illness can shape what kinds of solutions are offered in the film. By examining key films that take as their subject one kind of illness or impairment, as well as their reception and impact, we can see these changing approaches to illness in American society over the 20th century and into the 21st century.

INDIVIDUAL PROBLEMS, SOCIAL IMPACTS

Movies that portrayed problems with alcohol addiction were among the earliest and most common social problem films in the United States. Just one year into the 20th century, *The Victims of Alcohol* (1901) appeared. Scholar Kay Sloan calls this film and other films about alcoholism from the Progressive Era "temperance melodramas." These films coexisted with an active temperance movement, which advocated refraining from alcohol consumption. The movement culminated in the 18th Amendment to the US Constitution, which prohibited the manufacture and sale of alcohol. Ratified in 1919, national prohibition was a Progressive reform. Sloan summarizes the plots of many of these temperance melodramas. "Barroom brawls, scorned wives, abandoned children, jobs lost to drunkenness, but eventual remorse and a vow to 'lead the straight path' formed the essence of a host of moving pictures."[1] The focus of these films was the devastating effects of men's alcoholism on the family; women and children, not the drinker himself, were the primary victims of the "demon drink." For the most part, the narrative ended in a happy resolution with the father embracing a life of temperance.

Two examples of these temperance melodramas are the shorts *What Drink Did* (1909) and *A Drunkard's Reformation* (1909) by pioneering filmmaker D. W. Griffith. Lasting about 10 minutes each, these two movies present the dire consequences of the fathers' drinking and their eventual decision to give up alcohol. At the start, both show families divided by drink, with men in saloons and mothers with their children at home. In *What Drink Did*, the father is drinking in a saloon with his friends when his wife sends their daughter to fetch him. He rebuffs her violently, pushing her away. The daughter tries once more, and in the altercation that follows, she is shot by the saloon waiter and dies. "What drink did" was cause the tragic death of a child. A child is also central to the plot of *A Drunkard's Reformation*. The turning point in the story is when the father attends a temperance play with his daughter while his wife stays and prays at home. This play (within the movie) about a drunkard (based on Emile Zola's *L'Assommoir*) changes the father's perspective. "As the melodrama unfolds, a gnawing certainty grows within him," one title reads. He realizes he also has a problem with alcohol and vows to abstain. "A timely message! His own shortcomings mirrored in the stageplay," states another title.

Both movies end with the family members—at least those still alive!—reunited, as the "preservation of marriage and the family was the central theme" of temperance films.[2] The closing shot in *A Drunkard's Reformation* shows father, mother, and daughter gathered together in tableaux in the warm glow of the hearth, a fitting final image for a Griffith film. The narrative and its resolution in both films presented the cause and solution to alcoholism as within men's control. Their weakness for drink could be overcome with determination, and the flawed protagonist would be redeemed. This analysis reflected Victorian morals and manners rather than the new sociological thinking emerging with Progressivism. The vast majority of temperance melodramas did the same, but Sloan found an exception: *The Weaker Mind* (1913). This film suggested that alcoholism was a hereditary genetic disease rather than a moral failing, so the drunkard was more a victim rather than a perpetrator.[3] In Griffith's films, the women and children are the victims, the moral message clear, and the didacticism explicit. In opening titles for the films, Biograph Studios promoted *A Drunkard's Reformation* as "the Most Powerful Temperance Lesson Ever Depicted" and *What Drink Did* as "a Thoughtful Moral Lesson." In turn, temperance organizations used both films to rally support for their cause, demonstrating again the way early cinema could be marshaled for moral uplift.

The moral suasion of the Progressive Era social problem film erodes over time but was not completely erased in a film like *The Lost Weekend* (1945). Directed by Billy Wilder and starring Ray Milland as the alcoholic writer Don Birnam, this multiple Oscar–winning film tracks the protagonist through a disastrous weekend-long drinking binge. He is arrested, remanded to the alcoholic wing of Bellevue Hospital (nicknamed "Hangover Plaza"), suffers from delirium tremens, and contemplates suicide. Despite his many appalling actions and their negative social impact, these awful experiences evoke sympathy, and the film has a happy ending with Birnam cured. This tidy resolution revised the bleak ending of the original 1944 novel of the same name. "If the drunk wasn't . . . a hell of a nice guy and wanted to be saved, the audience wouldn't go for it," observed the head of Paramount to Wilder.[4] Most significantly, *The Lost Weekend* located Birnam's alcoholism in psychology, specifically his deep feelings of insecurity. This explanation for the causes of his addiction reflected the popular psychology of the 1940s and 1950s. Psychological ideas, like those of Sigmund Freud, proliferated in American popular culture and everyday life, due in part to their prominence in Hollywood movies. Although 10 years would pass before alcoholism was officially defined as a "disease," *The Lost Weekend*'s portrayal of psychological rather than moral causes for addiction constituted an advance in understanding. The movie reflected "modern medicine," stated Bosley Crowther in the *New York Times*, and offered "a forward, scientific viewpoint on excessive drinking."[5]

Yet the plot of *The Lost Weekend* left it up to Birnam, prompted by his fiancée (Jane Wyman), to recover on his own, without medical treatment. Such would not be the case with *When a Man Loves a Woman* (1994), where the alcoholic Alice Green (Meg Ryan) enters a medical rehabilitation center to recover and then attends regular meetings of Alcoholics Anonymous (AA). This movie makes it clear that alcohol-use disorder (now the preferred term over *alcoholism* or *alcohol abuse*) is a disease requiring both medical treatment and emotional support. It also hints at a hereditary genetic cause, like *The Weaker Mind*, as Alice Green's father was also an alcoholic. This message is undercut, however, in her final speech at an AA meeting when she describes herself as "low and weak." Still, *When a Man Loves a Woman* innovates by featuring a woman alcoholic—although the 1947 film *The Smash-Up*, considered a woman's version of *The Lost Weekend*, and *Days of Wine and Roses* (1962) did as well. It further introduces the concept of codependency. The experience of Alice's husband, Michael Green, is as much a focus of the film as her experience. "I'm not your problem to solve," she tells him, but he feels it is. Critic Roger Ebert noted that alcoholism is now understood to be a "disease of denial" and a "family disease" and that *When a Man Loves a Woman* shows that.[6]

Teaching Ideas

Fortunately, all of these movies and many other teaching materials are easily available online, at libraries, or for purchase.

- Griffith's *What Drink Did* (www.youtube.com/watch?v=jIJPH32WOTE) and *A Drunkard's Reformation* (www.youtube.com/watch?v=PrY43xlFT0M). These shorts are ideal for classroom use, and students can discuss both the message and meaning of these films, as well as the technique. In these films, Griffith was working out his film style. His editing included cross-cutting between simultaneous actions and to convey reaction (an early shot–reverse shot), as when the father in *A Drunkard's Reformation* comes to realize he has a problem. Attention to technique and the narrative structure of these films demonstrates how film art was progressing.
- Pair the movie shorts with selections on these films from the *Biograph Bulletin* in Paolo Cherchi Usai, ed., *The Griffith Project, Volume 2: Films Produced January–June 1909* (London: British Film Institute, 1999), 57–58 and 124–25. These selections provide plot summaries and explain the movies' messages. Their heightened language—"no stronger nor intensely moral sermon has ever been given"—conveys how filmmakers sought to promote their movies.
- Several useful teaching ideas for *The Lost Weekend* (1945) can be based on Chris Cagle's discussion of the formal strategies used in the film to convey its message and meaning, as well as its realism and social context. He highlights the opening, establishing shot of the New York City skyline, which pans down to show a liquor bottle hanging outside Don Birnam's apartment. The film's conclusion then repeats but reverses the opening shot, panning from the bottle outside to the skyline. Ray Milland's voice-over narration reinforces the idea that alcoholism is a social, not just an individual, problem. "And out there in the concrete jungle, I wonder how

many others there are like me." Cagle points out additional sequences, including a montage of Birnam walking the city streets and when he is at Bellevue Hospital. Both involved location shooting and reinforced the film's narrative (Birnam's descent) and critique (of inadequate medical treatment).[7]
- As with movie posters discussed in chapter 4, movie trailers are also promotional paratexts and "sell and tell" the narrative.[8] The trailers for *The Lost Weekend* (www.youtube.com/watch?v=j-tefK9hkuM) and *When a Man Loves a Woman* (www.youtube.com/watch?v=R6oxB257a7Q) are available online and can be used to see how the filmmakers sell and tell their movie. With *The Lost Weekend*, note the foregrounding of the original Charles Jackson novel, as well as reviews of the film. How does this market the movie as a "prestige picture"? With *When a Man Loves a Woman*, note how the opening voiceover is provided by Andy Garcia and how often he appears onscreen in the trailer. Combined with the title of the film and Garcia appearing first in the credits, rather than Meg Ryan, consider who is really the subject of the film. Why is the female character suffering from addiction marginalized? Remember that this film was released in 1994, a period of feminist backlash, as discussed in chapter 4.
- A compare-and-contrast analysis of one very positive and one very negative review of *When a Man Loves a Woman* by two very prominent film critics can be a basis for a good discussion of the film's message and meaning. Roger Ebert endorsed this "wise and ambitious film"[9] and David Denby dismissed this "pushy therapeutic exercise."[10] Who do you agree with, and why? What evidence do they provide for their arguments? Does the knowledge that Ebert was a recovering alcoholic add anything to your conclusions?
- The narratives for all of these films—the temperance melodramas, *The Lost Weekend*, and *When a Man Loves a Woman*—involves the sufferer hitting rock bottom before beginning the journey of recovery. What message does that send? This dramatic arc has been criticized by commentators for sending the wrong message, as recovery can and should be encouraged to begin at any point.

INSTITUTIONALIZING MENTAL ILLNESS

Two social problem films about mental illness provide the opportunity to discuss past approaches to the treatment for mental illness and what has changed since. *The Snake Pit* (1948) and *One Flew Over the Cuckoo's Nest* (1975) portrayed institutional settings for mentally ill patients. Institutionalization initially emerged as a solution to the problem of mental illness in the 19th century as a way to protect society *from* the sufferers, but more humane and rehabilitative approaches *toward* sufferers held sway during different historical movements. These different attitudes toward the institutional care of the victims of mental illness appeared in the plots and characters of *The Snake Pit* and *One Flew Over the Cuckoo's Nest*. Both of these social problem films had an impact on the public discussion of mental illness and how it should be managed in the 20th century. They signaled an advance in popular perceptions of mental illness over earlier views of mental illness as caused by supernatural forces, immorality, or physical disorders. Yet these movies still demonstrated the profound limits of medical and social understandings in the United States at the time of their production and reception.

The Snake Pit starred Olivia de Havilland as Virginia Cunningham, who has a nervous breakdown and is institutionalized. Upon its release in 1948, the film was frequently compared to *The Lost Weekend* in terms of its social problem genre and hard-hitting realism. It depicted Cunningham's harrowing experience in Juniper Hill State Hospital, an asylum based on New York's Rockland Hospital. Her involuntary commitment included time in Ward 12, called "the snake pit," a ward overcrowded with the most ill patients in the most inhumane conditions. The film combined this critique with sympathy for Cunningham's suffering. Her mental illness is treated by a psychiatrist with the latest medical treatments, including electroshock therapy, hydrotherapy, and psychotropic drug therapy, as well as psychoanalysis. In the end, she is cured, released, and returns home. Like *The Lost Weekend*, the movie was based on a best-selling book. Mary Jane Ward's 1946 novel adapted her own experience with mental illness and presented her point of view. But the male screenwriters added the perspective of a male psychiatrist, a move that undermined that of the female protagonist, as scholar Leslie Fishbein convincingly argues. They also redefined the source of Cunningham's mental illness to be an unresolved Oedipal complex or father fixation in keeping with popular Freudian psychology. Fishbein believes these changes indicated greater interest on the filmmakers' part in the "social problem caused by the tensions of modern womanhood rather than the crisis in mental health care."[11]

But the filmmakers promoted the film as about the latter, and contemporary respondents received it that way too. It helped that mental health was a prominent public issue following World War II. The National Mental Health Act in 1946 provided federal funding for mental health services for the very first time. It also helped that the producer of *The Snake Pit*, Darryl F. Zanuck of 20th Century-Fox, had a reputation in the social problem film genre from his work on *Gentleman's Agreement* (a film discussed in chapter 5). He and the director, Anatole Litvak, sought social reform. According to Litvak, their purpose was to "awaken public interest in this vital matter, to reassure people that mental disorder is an illness which can be cured, and to direct attention to the facilities now available in our institutions."[12] *The Snake Pit* was not alone in this aim. It joined an explosion of journalistic exposés about conditions in the nation's mental hospitals, as did other Hollywood movies. But as a prestige film, it had greater reach. "[I]t has the impact of a sledge hammer," concluded the *Chicago Tribune*'s Mae Tinee, "a modern tragedy which is a challenge to our claims to being civilized."[13] "This is, indeed, the living hell of human life," observed Edwin Schallert in the *Los Angeles Times*. "Above all this should lead to the goal of perpetually better care for these unfortunates."[14] Zanuck later credited his film with spurring legislation reforming mental hospitals in 26 states.[15]

When *One Flew Over the Cuckoo's Nest* was released in 1975, Americans were living in the wake of the social and cultural change of the 1960s and 1970s, which included mental health care reform. The documentation of abuses in state psychiatric hospitals, like those depicted in *The Snake Pit*, meant institutionalization was no longer considered right or humane. In the fields of medicine or sociology, institutionalization definitely was no longer considered to be the solution to the problem of mental illness. Public policy changed as a result. With the passage of the Community Mental Health Centers Act of 1963, many patients moved from state psychiatric hospitals to community-based facilities. The aim was to improve the medical treatment and living conditions for the mentally ill, and over the 1960s, the number of institutionalized patients dropped dramatically. Deinstitutionalization also altered social understandings of mental illness. *One Flew Over the Cuckoo's Nest* was set in 1963, the same year as the act's passage, and served to justify deinstitutionalization. Based on Ken Kesey's 1962 novel of the same name, the movie told the story of Randle P. McMurphy (Jack Nicholson), who feigns insanity in order to transfer to the state mental hospital from prison and a required work detail.

McMurphy rebels against the constraints and conditions of the psychiatric hospital, which pursues a custodial rather than rehabilitative approach, with many of the patients heavily medicated. He also refuses to accept the authority of Nurse Ratched (Louise Fletcher), the rigid and cruel head psychiatric nurse. As a portrayal of a woman in power, the role of Nurse Ratchet was very much shaped by the sexism of the early 1960s, when the original novel was published, the movie was set, and before the second wave of feminism began. McMurphy's audacity and antics win over the other patients, who display their essential humanity despite their inhumane environment. But in the process, the doctors deem him dangerous—even if he is not insane—and detain him in the hospital. Over the course of the movie, he is treated with electroshock therapy and eventually tragically lobotomized to make him more "manageable." One of his fellow patients smothers him with a pillow in what is considered an act of mercy. *One Flew Over the Cuckoo's Nest* reflected the era's antiauthoritarian mood. It was the highest-grossing film of 1976 and won all five major Academy Awards. Commentators saw in the movie reasons to support the new community-based approaches to mental illness. "In watching the movie," one sociologist observed, "the viewer cannot help but consider that perhaps the residents' needs might better be served in a humanized, noninstitutional setting."[16]

Teaching Ideas

As with other films discussed, these movies are available online, in libraries, or for purchase as DVDs.

- Promotional paratexts, including posters and trailers, are available online. The trailers for *The Snake Pit* (www.youtube.com/watch?v=1CBLJoNETqU) and *One Flew Over the Cuckoo's Nest* (www.youtube.com/watch?v=2WSyJgydTsA) provide useful information about how filmmakers are marketing their movies. Like *The Lost Weekend*, *The Snake Pit* is clearly a prestige picture with a serious tone, whereas *One Flew Over the Cuckoo's Nest* appears to be a more iconoclastic film with a comedic tone. Considering the historical and industrial contexts within which these films were made—the waning of the old Hollywood studio system and the waxing of New Hollywood—helps to explain these differences.
- Both of these movies are adaptations of novels, and it is useful to consider how the films differ from the original novels. This compare-and-contrast analysis can help to reveal the aims of filmmakers in bringing these stories from page to screen. Leslie Fishbein's article is a comprehensive guide to the changes with *The Snake Pit* and particularly what those changes tell us about Hollywood's representations of women in the post–World War II period.[17] The film version of *One Flew Over the Cuckoo's Nest* loses the hallucinatory scenes of the novel, and McMurphy's prison sentence for the rape of an underage girl is softened in the movie when he claims she said she was 18. But author Ken Kesey was angered by one fundamental change in the film version: the elimination of the narrator. In the book, the narrator is the Native American character, Chief Bromden. Since he no longer controls or frames the narrative, the character is reduced in importance in the film. Yet Chief Bromden remains a key figure in the movie. He is the one who kills McMurphy, and the final scene is of his long-awaited escape. He uses a hydrotherapy machine to break through a window—thus converting an instrument and symbol of his confinement to the opposite purpose—and runs away into the distance. When the film fades to black, the audience is left with a feeling of relief that he has finally found his freedom.
- Both of these films are shot in a realist style and use film technique to convey the institutional settings of the psychiatric hospitals and the feel-

ings of powerlessness on the part of the characters. The most famous scene from *The Snake Pit* is a high-angle crane shot that shows Virginia Cunningham looking vulnerable as she is enclosed and engulfed in the hospital. In *One Flew Over the Cuckoo's Nest*, director Miloš Forman uses lighting and shadows to emphasize a sense of entrapment. Both films use a very dull, washed-out color palette inside the institutions.
- Both of these films appeared in periods of public policy change and mental health reform and contributed to public debates. How did these films reflect and affect the social and political context in which they were produced and received? Although *The Snake Pit* reinforces faith in psychiatry as a profession and treatment, such faith is severely challenged in *One Flew Over the Cuckoo's Nest*. Indeed, the latter film raises questions about what "insanity" is or how to define it, questions that fit the context of the 1970s as a disability rights movement organizes to join the era's kaleidoscope of movements.

CHALLENGING THE SOCIAL STIGMA OF ILLNESS

With many illnesses, social stigma attaches to the sufferers. They are seen as different from the rest of us and as not fitting in with society. Hollywood has addressed this issue of perceived deviance in many social problem films, including films that take illness as a subject. Particularly interesting is when these films define social stigma, rather than the illness itself, as the social problem. Two examples are *The Best Years of Our Lives* (1946) and *Philadelphia* (1993). These films again demonstrate the hybridity of the social problem film genre. *The Best Years of Our Lives* fits the genre. Its subject is the experience of veterans coming home from combat in World War II and the individual and social problems they face in readjusting to civilian life. But it can also be considered a war film and a family melodrama. Similarly, *Philadelphia* addresses the problems faced by patients with AIDS (Acquired Immune Deficiency Syndrome), in this case a gay man. Yet it also takes the form of a courtroom drama and a biopic. These generic "ambiguities" or "overlap," to use Steve Neale's terms, did not undermine their reception as social problem films, however.[18]

Both films were considered very relevant within their historical contexts. The issue of veteran readjustment in 1946 remained pertinent the year after the end of World War II. Samuel Goldwyn, the producer of *The Best Years of Our Lives*, initiated the film project after being inspired by a news article about returning veterans in *Time* magazine in 1944. The movie tells the story of three veterans. Al Stephenson is middle-aged, with a wife of 20 years and a family, and he returns to his career in banking. Fred Derry is young, and his wartime marriage is on the rocks. After a frustrating search for employment—"All I want is a good job," he bemoans—he settles for his prewar job in a drug store. Homer Parrish is also young, and he is returning to his fiancée. But he has lost both of his hands and fears the pity of loved ones and stigma from society. This range of challenges—physical, personal, professional, and psychological—presented in the film were considered to be representative of those faced by US veterans as a whole. "And that is immediately important," contended the *New York Times*.[19] *Philadelphia*'s portrayal of the profound adversities faced by an AIDS patient also mattered very much in 1993, when an effective treatment emerged but coexisted with outright bigotry and discrimination. The plot focuses on an increasingly ill lawyer, played by Tom Hanks, who sues his law firm when they illegally fire him after discovering he is gay and has AIDS. The film conveyed "the full urgency of its difficult subject," concluded one reviewer.[20]

Attention to the contemporary relevance and urgent address of these films accompanied positive reception for their characters and realism. *The Best Years of Our Lives* and *Philadelphia* both evoked sympathy for their main characters. Tom Hanks's character was described by one reviewer as "a spiritually evolved human being—just, forgiving and kind."[21] Critic Janet Maslin complimented Hanks for performing this role with realism and "simple grace." His "transformation from robust lawyer to visibly suffering AIDS patient will not soon be forgotten."[22] Yet not all respondents considered *Philadelphia*'s depiction of a gay man and his partner convincing. There were hints of their sexuality, but gay filmgoers, it was reported, "wished for more such doses of reality."[23] The starring actors in *The Best Years of Our Lives* all won recognition for sympathetic portrayals, as occurred in the *Los Angeles Times*. That Harold Russell, who played Homer Parrish, was a real-life amputee made his performance "a deeply wrought thing—the most moving and central development in the plot."[24] A scene where Fred Derry (Dana Andrews) visits a military junkyard served as a poignant metaphor: his skills as an air force bombardier are now as useless as the airplanes themselves. A high-angle shot renders Derry small and alone among the abandoned military machines, a "man that was big in the service, who can't rise to that estate in civilian life." Overall, *The Best Years of Our Lives* was lauded as "a sound, solid, real impression of life."[25]

Finally, the lessons about confronting social stigma made explicit in the narratives of these two films were well received. *The Best Years of Our Lives* has a happy ending, with a memorable double wedding. Homer Parrish confronts and overcomes his fear of pity and stigma and marries his fiancée, Wilma. At the same time, in typical Hollywood fashion, Fred Derry, fresh from his divorce, conveniently falls in love and weds Peggy, Al Stephenson's daughter. For some contemporary as well as later commentators, the film provided the easy resolution of individual, romantic solutions to what are public problems. However, social and political concerns raised in *The*

Best Years of Our Lives did not disappear at the movie's end but stayed with filmgoers. This result was sought by the politically liberal director, William Wyler, and his team, but it also led to criticism by political conservatives just as the Hollywood blacklist began. Although Tom Hanks's character in *Philadelphia* dies in the end, he has won his legal case. It cannot be said the film has a happy ending, but there is a clear victory against bigotry and fear and for justice and acceptance. Even the learning attained by his lawyer, played by Denzel Washington, symbolizes this victory. In keeping with the aims of director Jonathan Demme and the arguments of AIDS activists, the movie demonstrated that AIDS was not just an individual medical problem but a social one. Collective solutions were necessary, including public health, education, and funding initiatives.

Teaching Ideas

Again, these movies are available online, in libraries, or for purchase as DVDs. Their posters and trailers, newspaper and internet reviews all can be used to ascertain aspects of their production and reception within their historical context.

- Both films have ironic titles and offer an opportunity to discuss the importance of film titles for promotion, as well as changing styles in film titles over time. How do the titles of films convey their message and meaning? *The Best Years of Our Lives* can be variously interpreted. Perhaps the best years of these men's lives were their wartime experiences, or did they give up the best years of their lives to combat? Most hopeful, perhaps their best years are to come. *Philadelphia* is the setting of the movie, but the city is also known as the "City of Brotherly Love." The movie expresses anger and frustration with the lack of communal feeling toward gay people and AIDS patients, as well as hope for the possibility of its realization with awareness and knowledge.
- *The Best Years of Our Lives* is a coming home from World War II film, but it can be usefully compared and contrasted with coming-home films from other US wars. The US war in Vietnam yielded several such films, including *Coming Home* (1978) and *Born on the Fourth of July* (1989). *In the Valley of Elah* (2007) is a coming home film from the US war in Iraq. Films from all these wars demonstrate soldiers' traumatic experiences of war and the lasting physical, emotional, and psychological effects, including post-traumatic stress disorder (PTSD). But what difference does the specific war make to the story being told in these various films? As discussed in chapter 1, World War II was understood as a "good war," but that is not the case with the US wars in Vietnam and Iraq. How does this

difference affect the films' portrayals of the experiences of soldiers and veterans?
- While *Philadelphia* is notable for being the first big-budget, mainstream, star-powered Hollywood film about AIDS, there are movies that predate it and many more that came after it. The later films deal both with AIDS and the virus that causes it, HIV (Human Immunodeficiency Virus). For many HIV-positive people, AIDS patients, as well as gay filmgoers, these other movies are much truer to their own lives and experiences. *Out* magazine (www.out.com/movies/2016/9/07/26-films-about-hivaids-everyone-should-watch) has a list of recommendations of early and later films that would provide a good opportunity for a compare-and-contrast analysis.

NOTES

1. Kay Sloan, *The Loud Silents: Origins of the Social Problem Film* (Urbana: University of Illinois Press, 1998), 1.
2. Ibid., 95.
3. Ibid., 96.
4. Buddy Da Silva, quoted in Peter Roffman and Jim Purdy, *The Hollywood Social Problem Film: Madness, Despair and Politics from the Depression to the Fifties* (Bloomington: Indiana University Press, 1981), 258.
5. Bosley Crowther, "Alcohol and Celluloid," *New York Times*, December 9, 1945, 53.
6. Roger Ebert, "*When a Man Loves a Woman*," RogerEbert.com, May 6, 1994, www.rogerebert.com/reviews/when-a-man-loves-a-woman-1994.
7. Chris Cagle, *Sociology on Film: Postwar Hollywood's Prestige Commodity* (New Brunswick, NJ: Rutgers University press, 2017), 82–87.
8. Lisa Kernan, *Coming Attractions: Reading American Movie Trailers* (Austin: University of Texas Press, 2004); Jonathan Gray, *Show Sold Separately: Promos, Spoilers, and Other Media Paratexts* (New York: New York University Press, 2010).
9. Ebert, "*When a Man Loves a Woman*."
10. David Denby, "A Vodka Tonic," *New York Magazine*, May 9, 1994, 66.
11. Leslie Fishbein, "*The Snake Pit* (1948): The Sexist Nature of Sanity," *American Quarterly* 31 (Winter 1979): 657.
12. Anatole Litvak, quoted in Thomas M. Pryor, "Of Litvak and the 'Pit,'" *New York Times*, November 7, 1948, X5.
13. Mae Tinee, "'The Snake Pit' Is Powerfully Done on Screen," *Chicago Daily Tribune*, November 16, 1948, A7.
14. Edwin Schallert, "'Snake Pit' Powerful Film Event," *Los Angeles Times*, December 27, 1948, 15.
15. Roffman and Purdy, *Hollywood Social Problem Film*, 261.
16. Daniel K. Quinn, review of *One Flew Over the Cuckoo's Nest*, directed by Miloš Forman, *Teaching Sociology* 17 (January 1989): 122.
17. Fishbein, "*Snake Pit* (1948)."
18. Steve Neale, *Genre and Hollywood* (London and New York: Routledge, 2000), 125–26.
19. "Homecoming Soldiers," *New York Times*, December 11, 1946, 30.
20. Janet Maslin, "Tom Hanks as an AIDS Victim Who Fights the Establishment," *New York Times*, December 22, 1993, C18.
21. Rita Kempley, "Movies: The 'Philadelphia' Story: A Case of Convictions," *Washington Post*, January 14, 1994, G1.
22. Maslin, "Tom Hanks as an AIDS Victim," C18.

23. David DeNicolo, "Is 'Philadelphia' on Target in Its Portrait of Gay Life?" *New York Times*, January 16, 1994, H22.

24. Edwin Schallert, "'Best Years of Lives' Saga of Home-Coming," *Los Angeles Times*, December 26, 1946, A3.

25. Ibid., A3.

WORKS CITED

Cagle, Chris. *Sociology on Film: Postwar Hollywood's Prestige Commodity*. New Brunswick, NJ: Rutgers University Press, 2017.

Fishbein, Leslie. "*The Snake Pit* (1948): The Sexist Nature of Sanity." *American Quarterly* 31 (Winter 1979): 641–65.

Gray, Jonathan. *Show Sold Separately: Promos, Spoilers, and Other Media Paratexts*. New York: New York University Press, 2010.

Kernan, Lisa. *Coming Attractions: Reading American Movie Trailers*. Austin: University of Texas Press, 2004.

Neale, Steve. *Genre and Hollywood*. London and New York: Routledge, 2000.

Quinn, Daniel K. Review of *One Flew Over the Cuckoo's Nest*, directed by Miloš Forman. *Teaching Sociology* 17 (January 1989): 122.

Roffman, Peter, and Jim Purdy. *The Hollywood Social Problem Film: Madness, Despair and Politics from the Depression to the Fifties*. Bloomington: Indiana University Press, 1981.

Sloan, Kay. *The Loud Silents: Origins of the Social Problem Film*. Urbana: University of Illinois Press, 1998.

Chapter Seven

Crime at the Movies

One of the arguments developed throughout this volume involves how social problem films drew upon other Hollywood genres, creating new kinds of hybrids that addressed these other recognizable structures through the social problem framework and mode of address. That framework sought to achieve a level of topicality and relevance and to do so seriously and sincerely. At the same time, this book has tried to model a process that puts its own ideas to the test. The crime and gangster film, which can operate as a subgenre of the social problem film, is the grouping of films that puts to the test this notion that social problem films are somehow distinct from the other Hollywood genres from which the social problem film draws. Of all the iterations of its broader genre, the social problem film's crime and gangster cycle arguably functions most independently and autonomously from its origins.

A great deal of popular and academic criticism, much of it early on, treated the gangster film as an entity in its own right, both in terms of its narrative motifs and in its iconography. Like other traditional genres, there are a clear set of narrative and formal attributes interacting with one another that make the crime film easy to identify and easy for distributors to categorize. Those might include the presence of a strong hero or ethnic antihero. There might be a tacked-on "crime doesn't pay" message at the end of the film. The setting might frequently take place in cramped urban spaces, speakeasies, penitentiaries, work camps, and other distinctive locales. Recognizable props might include guns, badges, uniforms, and the like. Special effects might emphasize gunplay, bloodletting, and explosions. Action might feature choreographed violence, high-speed car chases, or figurative movements and balletic expressions of death.

The magnitude of the crime and gangster movie genre exceeds the scope of this chapter. Not every crime and gangster movie functions as a social problem film in terms of its modality and how it asks us to take it seriously, its sense of urgency, its faith in social institutions to accommodate meaningful reform, and the like. Few would argue that *Bugsy Malone* (1976), a musical that substituted whipped cream for machine-gun bullets and was directed by Alan Parker with an all-child cast that included Jodie Foster and Scott Baio, functioned as a social problem film. It drew from the genre, recombining recognizable elements with the G-rated, family-friendly musical hybrid. Yet its hybrid worked, in part, because of audience facility with recognizable elements of the crime and gangster film that had developed over decades. That those elements eventually could function either nostalgically or parodically tells us something today about the life cycle of a genre and the audience literacy needed to understand the genre's readily accessible textual shortcuts that have emerged over time.

RECOGNIZING THE CYCLES OF CRIME AND GANGSTER FILMS

For the purposes of this chapter and its examination of crime in the social problem film, the focus will be on the trajectory from the early gangster film featuring a tragic or antiheroic figure to the gang films representing juvenile delinquency to the globalized crime films. Each of these cycles have significant overlap with one another. When Brian DePalma remade the main character in *Scarface* in 1983 as a Puerto Rican drug dealer, for example, a good 11 years had passed since Francis Ford Coppola released *The Godfather*. Coppola's franchise presaged the emergence of the globalized criminal syndicate films *Traffic* and *Syriana* in the 2000s.

Teachers and students might consider this trajectory as a kind of reflection within popular culture of the larger social fears and concerns regarding crime and criminals. This cycling also might tell us something about shifting social attitudes and sympathies. The gangster could be the social problem himself, produced by the forces of neglect, tenements, immigration, and urbanization. But the gangster also could emerge as the outsider and antihero, offering a contrapuntal commentary on middle-class values and blind faith in the American Dream. Gangster films of the 1930s, for example, offered a critique of consumption and materiality by presenting a mirror of the immigrant nouveau riche arriviste who got everything social mobility had to offer but did so just too quickly. And then there was the point of identification between the criminal and the law-abiding citizen. The gangster might be a family man or just a mama's boy who happens to commit heinous and violent crimes. Or the gangster might just as easily be a company man, if the company was Crime, Inc., and Crime, Inc., was just another corporation.

The crime film also had its progenitors within an ecosystem of popular texts, including newspaper and magazine muckraking accounts, dime detective novels, and the photojournalism of Lewis Hine and Weegee. Borne out of Progressive Era notions conflating bodily disease and infection with the putrid influences on the city, the genre negotiated negative connotations of immigrant hordes invading national borders and bringing with them cultural and social diseases. As cultural and social anxieties shifted, the films themselves shifted to address new fears of juvenile delinquency. And as social and economic systems began showing signs of weakness and inadequacy, the genre began to tackle white-collar crime and the consequences of institutional racism. With the rise of globalization, the genre embraced the paranoia of transnational and diffuse networks operating outside of governmental control and oversight.

While a comprehensive overview of the crime and gangster film is beyond the scope of this chapter, the chronological ordering of examples will attempt to model for teachers and students a best-practices approach to using these films to model critical and historical analysis using the social problem film genre. As discussed earlier, scholarly thinking and writing involves a series of steps, moving the reader through specific kinds of thinking and argument. Our analysis should include the following kinds of questions:

- What problem can an understanding of crime and gangster films as part of the social problem film genre solve?
- Why should teachers and students care about how these films depict gangsters and criminality?
- What kind of questions can we ask that the depictions from the crime and gangster social problem film can answer?
- How can the crime and gangster social problem film help students to better identify gaps in—as well as fundamental parallels with—the broader framework of assumptions we have about how the social problem film, and genre film in general, work?
- How can the crime and gangster social problem film help better identify gaps in our understanding, as well as parallels with what other people have said about these films?
- What kinds of questions can students and teachers ask that will help develop and extend a primary question or argument about crime and gangster social problem films?
- What evidence works best as a primary source that will help these supporting points, and how is this evidence different from secondary evidence?
- What new gaps or weaknesses in understanding about the crime and gangster social problem film have emerged as a result of your thinking and analysis?

While identification of a "problem" for looking at crime and gangster films might seem redundant—crime and gangsters are in fact the problem for social problem films—we once again should make the distinction between more generic problems, such as what to do about gangsters and criminality, and a problem that academic scholarship and analysis can solve. As discussed further, academic problems have certain attributes. First, the problem must be one that a broader community shares. If a student or a class lacks knowledge about the crime and gangster film, that may well be a problem that can be solved through further scholarship and analysis, but it is not necessarily a problem that is shared beyond the confines of that person or classroom. A problem must offer the potential for solutions that will contribute to greater and shared understandings beyond a few people or a single classroom. An individual could solve the problem of lacking knowledge about the crime and gangster film by educating him- or herself about the genre. But personal edification has not necessarily contributed to a greater or shared understanding of the genre that would benefit the larger community of those interested in that genre.

A problem for any genre film is how we know when the genre has moved from being a one-cycle wonder to having taken its shape. We know the social problem film in general has certain key features. These include its mode of address, the narrative's sense of urgency in finding a solution, its present tense, and its faith in social institutions to tackle the problem. But how do we know when the crime and gangster film mutated into the social problem film, or what Carlos Clarens called the social protest film?[1] The early 1930s marked what Peter Roffman and Jim Purdy deemed a prototypical cycle of gangster melodramas.[2] Four films in particular—*Little Caesar* (1930), *Public Enemy* (1931), *Scarface* (1932), and *I Am a Fugitive from a Chain Gang* (1932)—all had achieved tremendous popularity and attention. Yet Roffman and Purdy argued that only one—*I Am a Fugitive from a Chain Gang*—constituted the formation of the social problem film genre. The others constituted a prototypical cycle of films that led to the social problem film. Unlike *I Am a Fugitive*, those other films offered "implied social criticism" without giving way "to the exposés, commentaries, and inquiries of the problem film."[3]

Clarens's perspective differs from Roffman and Purdy's in defining when a group of films constitutes a genre and when it is a cycle. Clarens's book argued that *I Am a Fugitive* began a cycle of social protest within the crime film that had largely played out by the end of the 1930s. He interpreted the fatalism of these social protest films as a key attribute, which he suggested were essential to the expressionist style of later American film noir of the 1940s. Roffman and Purdy, on the other hand, argued that the gangster films of the early 1930s were the cycle leading to *I Am a Fugitive* and launched the social problem film as a genre. As a classroom exercise, consider the difference between a *cycle* and a *genre* for the crime and gangster film. What investment would Clarens's book have in seeing the social protest film as a cycle within the crime movie genre? Why would Roffman and Purdy look at the same films and conclude that the gangster cycle of the early 1930s was the precursor to the social problem film?

As discussed in previous chapters, we would want to ask why the debate between whether these films constitute a cycle or a genre would matter to an academic problem. Why should anyone care whether these were social protest films or precursors to another genre? Here again, the answer should have broader implications beyond one person's taste or inclinations. Perhaps more accurately, the question should be "Why should the broader community interested in such things care about this?" The answer to the "so what" question also should continue to lay the groundwork for further examination and analysis. If we understand the difference between a cycle and a genre, might there be a chance we could understand better how genres work by looking closely at one specific iteration of the social problem film and whether it spawned an entirely new genre? Do we gain deeper understanding into why the gangster cycle resonated so much with 1930s audiences? Can we better understand the historical context for these films and make informed connections to other factors, such as the Great Depression, the coming of sound in movies, and the relative freedom filmmakers enjoyed before the coming of industry self-censorship?

The answer to the "so what" question also should immediately build toward a tentative argument or research question that analysis and scholarship of the crime and gangster-oriented social problem film can answer. Because this kind of scholarship is not a court of law, a debate, or a science experiment in a laboratory, the premise of this question should not set out to prove something. We are not out to prove, for example, that the gangster films of the early 1930s comprised a cycle. Nor are we out to show something patently obvious, for example, that all gangster films of the early 1930s were shot in black and white. Rather, the tentative argument or research question is a kind of testing of the waters. We want to make some generalizable claims, ones that to the best of our knowledge no one else has tackled or ones that people think they know the answer to but actually don't understand the answer or some facet of the answer all that well. We also want to make a claim where two or more people might reasonably come to different conclusions or even disagree with one another.

READING CULTURAL VALUES THROUGH CRIME AND GANGSTER SOCIAL PROBLEM FILMS

Many influential analyses of gangster films have attempted to use the specifics of the gangster film to gain broader insights into the workings of culture at large. In his famous article, "The Gangster as Tragic Hero," Robert Warshow argued that "the gangster is doomed because he is under the obligation to succeed." Audiences, Warshow claimed, have ambivalent attitudes about success. "Every attempt to succeed is an act of aggression, leaving one alone and guilty and defenseless among enemies: one is *punished* for success." The gangster film ultimately relieves this tension between success and morality in the death of the gangster. "The dilemma is resolved," Warshow wrote, "because it is *his* death, not ours. We are safe; for the moment, we can acquiesce in our failure, we can choose to fail."[4]

Using Warshow's overarching premise—that the gangster serves as a scapegoat that ultimately resolves larger tensions between success and morality—we could test this idea with other, more recent examples. What other crime and gangster movies and television shows address this tension? In those examples, does the narrative end in the death of the gangster? Does the death end up resolving this tension? Ideally, this discussion could provide a range of examples that might parallel or contradict Warshow's thesis. If occurring in a class discussion, the instructor might ask the class to refine this thesis. *Some* gangster films resolve the tension between success and morality in the death of the gangster. Other films might resolve the tension with a metaphorical death. Or perhaps the formula is different for television shows like *The Sopranos* than it is for feature films, where the death of the gangster and his middle-class family remains shrouded in ambiguity, much to the consternation, even to this day, of some fans and critics.

We also can ask questions of the social problem film that can address larger texts that extend beyond just the social problem film. Returning to the star text, for example, we can take two key social problem films of the 1950s representing juvenile delinquency—*The Wild One* (1953) and *Rebel Without a Cause* (1955)—and ask questions of the stars of those films, Marlon Brando and James Dean, respectively. In what ways do these performances function as texts in their own right, both in and outside the films and genres? How do these star performances interface with the conventions of the social problem film? How do the gender and sexuality of the main stars fit within the conventions of the genre?

These kinds of questions do not occur in a vacuum but must relate back to an intellectual community that may already have examined some aspect of these star texts. Thus, these kinds of questions are only as good as the connections they are able to make to previous research and scholarship. In an earlier chapter, we considered Richard DeCordova's concept of intertextuality in relation to the star. But we also can study stars in other ways. In their case study on the role of the star in film history, for example, Robert C. Allen and Douglas Gomery used the work of Richard Dyer to ask how movie stars served as "social phenomena" and whether one can study a particular star "historically."[5] We might refine the question to ask, Can we study stars *in social problem films* as a social phenomenon? And how can we study stars *of social problem films* historically?

Because a lot of work already has been done on both Marlon Brando and James Dean as star texts cutting across multiple film performances, in publicity about the films, and in circulated and in some cases manufactured biographies, there is no need to reinvent the wheel. We know from Dyer that both Brando's and Dean's acting styles at the time achieved reputations for "subversive" performances, not just in terms of what constituted a more realistic masculine performance but also in terms of their homoeroticism.[6] In *The Wild One*, for example, there is an iconic production still of Brando in a leather biker jacket and cap. Dean's performances frequently emphasized the emotionally wounded nature of his characters, and the ambiguous orientation of his sexuality has been the subject of both popular and academic contestation.

If asking the right kind of question means seeking parallels with some of the scholarship on both Marlon Brando and James Dean that already has occurred, asking the right kind of question also means finding gaps in this work that your question seeks to fill. For example, how has this scholarship treated the star text as a feature of the social problem film and its depiction of juvenile delinquency? A search of secondary literature might uncover that there is a lot of academic scholarship on the cycle of juvenile delinquency operating throughout the 1950s in the social problem film genre and a respectable amount of scholarship detailing the star texts of both Brando and Dean. But there nonetheless is a gap in the existing scholarship that discusses how these star texts function within—or perhaps at odds with—the conventions of the cycle and genre.

If we were to assume that a gap in our understanding exists with regard to how the star text functions within the crime and gangster social problem film, we then can ask a basic question: What can the star text in the crime and gangster social problem film tell us about how stars function as a social phenomenon? Remember, we can assume that scholarship already exists on the juvenile delinquent cycle of the social problem film. And we know that there is scholarship on both Brando and Dean that discusses both their biographies and their acting styles. But in identifying the work that others already have done, our discussion of that work can point to the gap in the scholarship: there appears to be very little discussion here in terms of how these particular star texts functioned within the conventions of the social problem film. The rest of the premise then can develop this idea further by breaking down the question into smaller chunks. How did Brando's performance in *The Wild One* function as part of the film's overall depiction of juvenile delinquency? How did Dean's performance as a teenager alienated from his dysfunctional family fit within the film's social problem film conventions? What did reviews of the time say about these performances?

HOW CRIME AND GANGSTER SOCIAL PROBLEM FILMS SPEAK TO SOCIAL CRISES

Identifying a specific question to ask, one that isn't simply a rehash of what other scholarship already has covered, and then breaking that question down into smaller chunks that advance the central idea of the paper is one of the most challenging aspects of academic writing. However, once you develop this framework, you're really more than halfway there. Let's see if we can apply this process to a different pair of films and a different time. Only four years apart, both *Wall Street* (1987) and *Boyz n the Hood* (1991) were cultural benchmarks of the time. *Wall Street* came on the heels of a 1986 insider stock trading scandal, and the film encapsulated much of the cultural critique of 1980s greed and materialism that popular discourse saw as marking the decade. Gordon Gekko, the film's fictional antagonist, established a catchphrase for the decade with "greed is good." A few years later and following the phenomenal success of Spike Lee's *Do the Right Thing*, 23-year-old John Singleton directed *Boyz n the Hood*, a film about how a divorced father tries to raise his teenage son in the violent Crenshaw ghetto of South Central Los Angeles. Like *Wall Street*, it too came amid a major social flashpoint and crisis. In March 1991, George Halliday captured on video the police apprehension and beating of motorist Rodney King. The video was widely shown on television newscasts. Community and civic leaders in Los Angeles had been complaining about police harassment and use of excessive force against people of color for years but were unable to make much headway. Singleton's film was released in July 1991 to much acclaim as an authentic depiction of black life in Los Angeles. After a lengthy trial of the police officers involved in the King beating, a multiracial but mostly white jury acquitted the police officers. News of the verdict immediately led to the 1992 Los Angeles uprising at the end of April, immediately after Singleton had earned multiple Oscar nominations and was being hailed as the chronicler of a new wave of African American filmmaking.

The proximity and relevance of both films to actual moments of cultural crisis in American history should lead us to ask a specific question. We could modify our earlier question regarding star texts by asking how the crime and gangster social problem films speak to ongoing social crises as they unfold. But that question by itself a bit generalized. Perhaps we would want to ask how crime and gangster social problem films of the late 1980s and early 1990s spoke to the cultural crises of insider trading scandals and racial violence. Still somewhat broad, but in order to answer the "how" question, we can explore this central idea further with some tentative supporting points. *Wall Street* spoke to the capitalist excesses of the 1980s through a narrative built around a "ripped from the headline" story about amoral insider trading. *Boyz n the Hood* just happened to be released right around the time America's racial conflicts and divides were boiling over. Another point might offer a comparison and contrast between the two films. Did a film about white-collar crime operate according to a different set of narrative conventions from a film exposing the violence and disaffection of a Los Angeles ghetto?

If we were to develop these supporting points, we would want to think about what kind of evidence would help to do that. For identifying gaps in knowledge or a weakness in understanding that a new project proposes to fill, we would want to turn to secondary sources. These are sources, typically scholarly, that are once removed from the historical event discussed. A scholarly book or an article in an academic journal typically is used as a secondary source to show where more work on a subject needs to be done. Primary sources, on the other hand, belong to and come out of the historical moment. A close analysis of *Wall Street* or *Boyz n the Hood* would use elements from those films as primary evidence. For example, you could analyze closely how different elements of a scene from *Wall Street*—say lighting, editing, and camerawork—combine to offer a visual commentary on 1980s greed. Or you could study on-location camerawork and mise-en-scène to see how *Boyz n the Hood* offers a visual commentary of ghetto life in the 1990s.

For film analysis, however, primary evidence goes well beyond just the films themselves. Both *Wall Street* and *Boyz n the Hood* were important personal projects for their respective directors, Oliver Stone and John Singleton. Stone dedicated *Wall Street* to his father, who was a stockbroker. Singleton made his directorial debut when he was 23 years old, and in newspaper interviews, he admitted that he built the narrative around his personal experience growing up in South Central Los Angeles. Thus, interviews with directors, movie reviews that might mention these personal details, even advertising and publicity that emphasize the importance of the director to these films all could serve as primary evidence alongside analysis of the film itself. Such additional primary evidence can even help inform and enrich a close analysis, not exist at odds with it.

DVDs offer new possibilities for finding primary evidence and then using that evidence to match questions of more recent crime social problem films. The DVDs of *Traffic* (2000) and *Syriana* (2005), two films that address globalization and transnational crime, include extras and bonus disks. Both films follow the social problem genre convention of adapting source material in a different format. For example, writer Stephen Gaghan adapted *Traffic* from a British miniseries about the international drug trade in Afghanistan and China. Gaghan transplanted the plot to the US-Mexico border. For *Syriana*, which Gaghan also wrote and directed, the film is loosely based on Robert Baer's *See No Evil*, a 2003 *New York Times* best seller about the failure of American foreign policy to address globalized terror movements. If you wanted to learn more about how the scripts for these films might have made changes to better conform to the conventions of the social problem film, you could listen to the director's commentary track and watch deleted scenes and additional footage. In addition, trailers and coming attractions provide a wealth of evidence, since they often help establish and then nourish viewer expectations for what the movie will be, typically in just a few minutes.

Primary evidence frequently defies expectations or might feature contradictions. When this happens, students should welcome the opportunity to refine or even revise a supporting argument. The bonus features for *Syriana*, for example, offer contradictory statements about what the film tries to accomplish. Because film is a collaborative effort, such contradiction is frequently the case. The many different creative and technical people involved all might have a different conception of what their role is and how the final product should look. A featurette about producer-star George Clooney, for example, shows Clooney asserting that the film is not really political but more of a glimpse into the human side of people like Bob Baer involved in fighting terrorism. Clooney argues that Baer was simply a company man who became disillusioned by the downsizing of his organization, which happened to be the Central Intelligence Agency (CIA) and its overseas covert operations. Yet Clooney also makes the point that much of the intelligence failures depicted in the film resulted from repeated budget cuts to the CIA and how in order to fight terrorism, those budgets would need to be restored. Hardly an apolitical point from the film's star and executive producer. A different featurette, meanwhile, emphasizes the film's purpose in calling attention to our overdependence on oil, the threat that dependence holds for future generations, and how this dependence implicates the United States in worldwide terrorism and globalized criminal networks.

What can this supporting evidence tell us about the way *Syriana* operates as a social problem crime film? Despite the relatively new topic—globalization and transnational crime—the film actually follows conventions that are well established in the genre. It attempts to humanize a broader social problem and gain sympathy for the audience through well-drawn and delineated fictionalized characters. The social problem film is never just a social problem film but a social problem film plus something else. In this case, *Syriana* could double as a biopic about a former CIA agent. The featurette interviews illustrate the film's sense of purpose and urgency. Society needs to do something now to address this problem. Yet the problem is complex, and there are no easy solutions. Perhaps increased funding to the CIA will solve part of the problem. But a big part of the problem also is American dependence on oil. In the featurette, writer-director Stephen Gaghan talks about his ambivalence of being implicated in this system yet the enjoyment he gets from driving the muscle car he owns down the streets of Los Angeles. The film also manages to be topical without actually taking sides and becoming too political. This push-pull between the apolitical humanizing of the social problem film and the ways in which the genre attempts to navigate its landscape without becoming too radicalized is on full display in the DVD extras for this film.

NOTES

1. Carlos Clarens, *Crime Movies: An Illustrated History* (New York: Norton, 1980), 108–10.
2. Peter Roffman and Jim Purdy, *The Hollywood Social Problem Film: Madness, Despair, and Politics from the Depression to the Fifties* (Bloomington: Indiana University Press, 1981), 16.
3. Ibid., 16.
4. Robert Warshow, "The Gangster as Tragic Hero," in *The Immediate Experience: Movies, Comics, Theatre and Other Aspects of Popular Culture*, enlarged ed. (Cambridge, MA: Harvard University Press, 2001), 103.
5. Robert C. Allen and Douglas Gomery, *Film History: Theory and Practice* (New York: Knopf, 1985), 172.
6. Richard Dyer, *Heavenly Bodies: Film Stars and Society*, 2nd ed. (New York: Routledge, 2004), 11.

WORKS CITED

Allen, Robert C. and Douglas Gomery. *Film History: Theory and Practice.* New York: Knopf, 1985.
Clarens, Carlos. *Crime Movies: An Illustrated History.* New York: Norton, 1980.
Dyer, Richard. *Heavenly Bodies: Film Stars and Society.* 2nd ed. New York: Routledge, 2004.
Roffman, Peter and Jim Purdy. *The Hollywood Social Problem Film: Madness, Despair, and Politics from the Depression to the Fifties.* Bloomington: Indiana University Pres, 1981.
Warshow, Robert. "The Gangster as Tragic Hero." In *The Immediate Experience: Movies, Comics, Theatre and Other Aspects of Popular Culture*, 97–104. Enlarged ed. Cambridge, MA: Harvard University Press, 2001.

DOCUMENTS

Social Problem Film Paper Sample Worksheet

What shared problem have I identified in scholarship on the social problem film, either a gap in our understanding that no one has talked about or a weakness in knowledge, something we think we know about but really don't?

How can I express this problem as one that is shared by a community (more than just me)? What existing published scholarship can I use to demonstrate that the gap in knowledge or weakness in understanding regarding the social problem film goes beyond just me?

So what? Why should this problem matter to classmates, to my teacher, or to a community of people outside my class who are interested in the social problem film?

How will my paper or project try to solve the problem I've identified? (e.g., a more recent film helps put older social problem films in context; close viewing of a social problem film will reveal something others haven't noticed before; historical evidence I have found about a social problem film gives new insight into the genre no one else noticed; etc.)? Do I have the evidence I need to solve the problem, and if not how can I get it?

What do I tentatively predict I'll find as I try to solve this problem (thesis or research question), and what are three specific points I can make to support this prediction and help me get to the solution?

    Prediction (Main Idea):

Supporting Points to Main Idea

1.

2.

3.

How will the first specific point contribute to solving the problem, what examples can I use, and how will my examples help build toward a solution?

How will the second specific point contribute to solving the problem, what examples can I use, and how will my examples help build toward a solution?

How will the third specific point contribute to solving the problem, what examples can I use, and how will my examples help build toward a solution?

What do I think will change, either in terms of new information or a better understanding of existing information, as a result of how I have attempted to solve the problem?

Sample Syllabus

Teaching History through Message Movies

DESCRIPTION

This course is designed to provide you with the opportunity to examine Hollywood feature films known as message movies, or social problem films, as historians, within the larger context of 20th and 21st century US social and cultural history. Organized chronologically, it situates the production and consumption of significant social problem films within their specific historical contexts and analyzes these films for what they can reveal about the conditions that produced them, attracted audiences to them, and shaped their reception.

OBJECTIVES

Course objectives are threefold: First, to acquire and expand knowledge of the history of the United States in the 20th and 21st centuries through Hollywood message movies; second, to further develop the skills of the historian, including thinking historically, marshalling evidence from primary, particularly film, and secondary sources and crafting historical interpretations; and third, to further develop proficiency in writing historical essays.

ASSIGNMENTS AND GRADING

1. Discussion Assignments (30%)
2. Midterm Paper (35%)

3. Final Paper (35%)

SCHEDULE OF TOPICS BY WEEK

1. Introduction to the Message Movie, or Social Problem Film

    Focus: What social problem films can tell us about the American past.
    Key Films: *What Drink Did* (1909) and *A Drunkard's Reformation* (1909)

2. Social Problem Films, 1910s

    Focus: Cinema and the "paradox" of Progressive politics and reform.
    Key Films: *Traffic in Souls* (1913) and *Cry of the Children* (1912)

3. Message Movies and the "Tribal Twenties," 1920s

    Focus: Film and conflicts over immigration and racial/ethnic relations in the Jazz Age.
    Key Films: *Within our Gates* (1920), *Hungry Hearts* (1922), and *Jazz Singer* (1927)

4. "Hard Times" for Celluloid Criminals, 1930s

    Focus: The popularity of the gangster genre complicating the criminal as "social problem."
    Key Films: *Public Enemy* (1931), *Scarface* (1932), and *I Am a Fugitive from a Chain Gang* (1932)

5. The Dark Side of the World War II Home Front, 1940s

    Focus: Hollywood's depictions of home-front social problems given wartime disruptions.
    Key Films: *Mildred Pierce* (1945), *The Lost Weekend* (1945), and *The Best Years of Our Lives* (1946)

6. Racial Liberalism under Fire, 1940s

    Focus: White liberal moviemakers challenging racial and ethnic prejudice.
    Key Films: *Crossfire* (1947), *Gentleman's Agreement* (1947), *Pinky* (1949), and *Home of the Brave* (1949)

7. "A Troubled Feast"? 1950s

    Focus: Movies construct the problem of juvenile delinquency in an age of consumerism.

Key Films: *The Wild One* (1953) and *Rebel Without a Cause* (1955)

8. Hollywood's Generation Gap, 1960s

    Focus: Filmic definitions of youth rebellion and generational/racial/gender conflict.
    Key Films: *Bonnie and Clyde* (1967), *Guess Who's Coming to Dinner* (1967), and *In the Heat of the Night* (1967)

9. Class and New Hollywood, 1970s

    Focus: Movie portrayals of class conflict in an age of deindustrialization.
    Key Films: *Rocky* (1976) and *Norma Rae* (1979)

10. Coming Home from the Vietnam War, 1970s–1980s

    Focus: Hollywood presents the problems of American veterans returning from war.
    Key Films: *Coming Home* (1978), *Deer Hunter* (1978), and *Born on the Fourth of July* (1989)

11. The American Dream in Crisis, 1990s

    Focus: Movies and social conflict at century's end.
    Key Films: *American Beauty* (1999) and *Crash* (2004)

12. The Price of the American Empire at Home and Abroad, 2000s

    Focus: Filmic depictions of global and US domestic social problems in the new century.
    Key Films: *Traffic* (2000), *Syriana* (2005), and *In the Valley of Elah* (2007)

WEEKLY DISCUSSION ASSIGNMENTS

You are expected to attend and participate in every discussion. To meet this expectation, the weekly lecture must be attended and required reading and viewing assignments must be completed before each meeting. Then you are expected to participate intelligently in discussion and activities.

Weekly discussion assignments are designed to enhance your learning of course content and skills with a focus on historical reception and primary-source research. These assignments aid your understanding of the historical and discursive contexts within which social problem films were produced, distributed, and consumed. You must complete a total of four (4) assignments of your choice during the course.

- Protest over *Birth of a Nation* (1915): Critics considered this film a social problem. Read two responses protesting this film on the website History Matters: "NAACP Official Calls for Censorship," http://historymatters.gmu.edu/d/4966, and "Reformer Jane Addams Critiques *The Birth of a Nation*," http://historymatters.gmu.edu/d/4994. In approximately 250 words, explain why these two historical figures launched their protests. What issues were at stake in their protests? Were their arguments persuasive? Can you imagine the content of a counterargument? What would it be?
- Youth and Movie Culture in the 1920s: Commentators feared young movie fans were becoming a social problem. Select two of the following four primary sources from Herbert Blumer's research on the History Matters website: "Kissing Rudy Valentino," http://historymatters.gmu.edu/d/21; "From Cowboys to Clara Bow," http://historymatters.gmu.edu/d/22; "Movie Dreams and Movie Injustices," http://historymatters.gmu.edu/d/23; "Frustration versus Fantasy," http://historymatters.gmu.edu/d/24. In approximately 250 words, reflect on how these sources demonstrate movies shaping the values and conduct of young people. What did Blumer's research reveal about the influence of movies on young people's ideas about life, how it should be lived, and what it offered them? What fears may have been prompted among observers from the revelations in these sources about youth culture and mass entertainment in the 1920s?
- Audience Reception and *Gone with the Wind* (1939): *Gone with the Wind* (1939) was the top US box office hit in the 1930s and for many years thereafter. Although not a social problem film and more accurately a historical epic, the correspondence around the film reveals much about the relationship between the Hollywood movie industry and its audience. Go to the Producing *Gone with the Wind* website, http://norman.hrc.utexas.edu/GWTW/#top, and read the Fan Mail Database overview. From there, under Browse, select either Suggestions, Preview Questionnaires, or Protests, and then read one featured story. In approximately 250 words, explain what the story tells us about how audiences received news about the making of *Gone with the Wind*. How do you explain their responses? Then look at Selznick Replies (under Fan Mail). What do you make of his and the studio's response to the fan mail?
- Culture, Power, and *Mission to Moscow* (1943): Historian Todd Bennett wrote an important article about the Hollywood film *Mission to Moscow* (1943) within the context of World War II. Although war films are usually considered a genre separate from the social problem film, there is often overlap between the two, especially when considering films about the home front or coming home. The controversy over *Mission to Moscow* reveals the discursive context in which the politics of all World War II films were debated. Go to this website: http://archive.oah.org/special-is-

sues/teaching/2001_09/index.html. Read the entire "Teaching the Article," and then examine the two cartoons from 1939 and 1943 hyperlinked in the third paragraph. Then choose two additional hyperlinked documents to read. In approximately 250 words, analyze what your two documents tell us about the film and/or its production and/or its reception and its significance during World War II.
- Reading Summary: Select a week's topic and, in approximately 250 words, write a summary of the main points of first reading and a list of at least three discussion questions. Your summary should include a statement of the author's arguments and your response. Do you agree/disagree with the author, and why? You will also write a list of at least three discussion questions for your classmates. A good discussion question prompts more than a "yes" or "no" answer, it helps students more deeply understand the reading and can ideally lead to debate.
- Journal Article Analysis: Select a week's topic and find a journal article on the same topic. Read the article and, in approximately 250 words, compare and contrast it with our required reading—that is, discuss similarities and differences in approach to the topic, argument, sources, and perspective of authors for the two articles.
- Film Review: Select a week's required film and find a contemporary review of the film. By *contemporary*, we mean from the time the film was made, not afterward. Then, in approximately 250 words, describe how the film was reviewed. Was it a positive or negative review? Were there any points made in the review that surprised or interested you? If you were to write a review, would it be similar or different? Why do you think that is the case?
- Current News Story Contextualization: Select a current news story about an issue in the United States relevant to the week's topic. In approximately 250 words, discuss the historical connections between how the issue was approached and understood in the past and how it is approached and understood today. What historical continuities and/or changes do you see?

MIDTERM PAPER ASSIGNMENTS

1. A paper of 1,000 words based upon a week's film, required reading, and recommended reading, including history textbooks, to answer the question: What can this source tell us about the people, society, and culture that created it? You do not need to address every aspect of "people, society, and culture" but can choose the observations you want to make. Be sure you use evidence drawn from the film and buttressed by historical evidence drawn from the required and recommended reading.

2. In this paper, you are expected to draw upon the film *The Jazz Singer* (1927), required reading, and recommended reading to answer the question: Although conflict is usually seen to best characterize racial and ethnic relations in the 1920s, to what extent does hybridity (cultural mixing and crossovers among white, African, and ethnic Americans) do so? Be sure you use evidence drawn from the film and buttressed by historical evidence drawn from the required and recommended reading.

FINAL PAPER ASSIGNMENTS

1. A paper of 2,000 words in which you present the case for the ways in which Hollywood message movies, and the meanings Americans attributed to them, either reflected or challenged (or both) dominant understandings of social problems in the 20th and 21st century in the United States. You are encouraged to select a theme or topic (social institutions and identities related to class, race and ethnicity, gender and the family, illness, and crime) around which to organize your paper.
2. A paper of 2,000 words in which you consider how social problem films called into question and/or support the possibility of the perfectibility of social institutions and identities in the 20th and 21st century in the United States. You are encouraged to select message movies related to a specific theme or topic (class, race and ethnicity, gender and the family, illness, and crime) around which to organize your essay.
3. A paper of 2,000 words in which you present an analysis of a social problem film using the Social Problem Film Paper Worksheet to guide your research, reading, and writing. The final paper will be evaluated on the basis of its relevance to the topic and to the genre of the social problem film; the substance and significance of your argument; how well the paper engages the concepts discussed; the thoughtfulness and originality with which the paper synthesizes these concepts; and the overall structure, readability, clarity, and the effectiveness of how the paper advances its argument.

Message Movies for Classroom Use

LABOR AND CLASS CONFLICT

Black Fury (1936). Directed by Fritz Lang. An immigrant is caught in a dispute between the owners of a coal mine and the union representing miners. DVD (Warner Home Video).

Blue Collar (1978). Directed by Paul Schrader. Auto workers plan a small-time robbery of their local union but discover a far deadlier system aligned against them. DVD (Universal Studios).

Born in Flames (1983). Directed by Lizzie Borden. After a socialist revolution fails to deliver on its promises and becomes increasingly violent, a group of women decide to take the revolution into their own hands. DVD (First Run Features); streaming.

Bound for Glory (1976). Directed by Hal Ashby. Biopic of the folk singer Woody Guthrie, who fought for victims of the Great Depression. DVD (MGM Home Entertainment).

Boxcar Bertha (1972). Directed by Martin Scorsese. A young woman joins a union leader and his gang, who rob trains to take revenge on the railroad. DVD (MGM Home Entertainment).

Capital Versus Labor (1910). Directed by Van Dyke Brooke. A clergyman and young officer vie for the daughter of successful manufacturer. No known distributor.

Cass Timberlane (1947). Directed by Clarence Brown. A well-to-do judge marries a working-class girl and discovers the hypocrisy of his social circle. DVD (Warner Home Video).

Children of Eve (1915). Directed by John H. Collins. A young woman with a shady past goes undercover to expose child labor and dangerous working conditions at a factory owned by the uncle of the social worker she loves. DVD (Kino).

Children Who Labor (1912). Directed by Ethel Browning. A wealthy businessman buys a factory that uses child labor, discovering that he has inadvertently enslaved his long-lost daughter. DVD (Image Entertainment).

Cradle Will Rock (1999). Directed by Tim Robbins. The behind-the-scenes story of producing Marc Blitzstein's leftist musical *Cradle Will Rock* in the 1930s. DVD (Touchstone Home Video).

The Crime of Carelessness (1912). Directed by Harold M. Shaw. Negligence on the part of a factory owner, safety inspector, and careless worker results in a deadly factory fire. DVD (Image Entertainment).

The Cry of the Children (1912). Directed by George Nichols. The film contrasts the ease of the rich family that owns the factory with impoverished child laborers, many of them appearing in actual footage working in a mill. DVD (Thanhouser Company Film Preservation).

The Deer Hunter. (1978). Directed by Michael Cimino. The Vietnam War has a devastating effect on the lives of ethnic Pennsylvania steelworkers and their families. DVD (Universal Studios Home Entertainment).

Edge of the City (1957). Directed by Martin Ritt. An interracial friendship between an army deserter and dockworker goes up against a bullying union racketeer. DVD (Warner Home Video).

Emperor of the North (1973). Directed by Robert Aldrich. A hobo goes up against a homicidal train conductor during the Great Depression. DVD (Twilight Time).

F.I.S.T. (1978). Directed by Norman Jewison. A charismatic Jimmy Hoffa–like union leader soon finds his links to organized crime to be his downfall. DVD, Blu-ray (Kino Lorber).

Give Us This Day (1949). Directed by Edward Dmytryk. Italian immigrant newlyweds find themselves trapped in the viciousness of a New York City tenement. DVD (Image Entertainment).

Gold Diggers of 1933 (1933). Directed by Mervyn LeRoy. Quintessential Depression-era backstage musical featuring the eye-popping "Forgotten Man" musical finale depicting the hardships of World War I veterans. DVD (Warner Home Video).

The Grapes of Wrath (1940). Directed by John Ford. Impoverished Okie farmers, forced off their land, travel to California during the Great Depression in search of a better life. DVD (20th Century Fox Home Entertainment).

Heroes for Sale (1933). Directed by William Wellman. A World War I hero turns around a drug addiction to become a successful capitalist whose efforts to implement factory automation unintentionally costs the lives of his workers. DVD (Warner Home Video).

I Can Get It for You Wholesale (1951). Directed by Michael Gordon. A former model tries to succeed in a male-dominated and cutthroat fashion industry, no matter what the costs. DVD (20th Century Fox Home Entertainment).

I Married a Communist aka *The Woman on Pier 13* (1949). Directed by Robert Stevenson. A shipping executive's former past as a Communist comes back to haunt him. DVD (Warner Home Video).

The Insider (1999). Directed by Michael Mann. Based on the true story of a tobacco industry whistleblower and the groundbreaking interview he gave to CBS's *60 Minutes*. DVD (Touchstone Home Video).

Kuhle Wampe or Who Owns the World? (1932). Directed by Slatan Dudow. Forced into desperate circumstances, a German working-class family loses their apartment and moves to a tent city outside Berlin before their daughter becomes radicalized and joins a worker youth movement. DVD (Icestorm Entertainment).

Make Way for Tomorrow (1937). Directed by Leo McCarey. An elderly couple experiencing financial hardship finds themselves shunned by their successful but selfish adult children. DVD (Criterion).

Matewan (1987). Directed by John Sayles. A violent West Virginia coal mining company exploits its labor in dangerous working conditions during the 1920s. DVD (PDX); streaming.

Metropolis (1927). Directed by Fritz Lang. A robot masquerading as a labor organizer further divides a futuristic city already deeply divided along class lines. DVD (Kino).

Modern Times (1936). Directed by Charlie Chaplin. Two social outcasts struggle to survive together within a highly mechanized and stratified society. DVD (Criterion).

Norma Rae (1979). Directed by Martin Ritt. A single mother joins forces with a labor organizer to unionize the factory where she works. DVD (20th Century Fox Home Entertainment).

One Third of a Nation (1939). Directed by Dudley Murphy. A slum landlord falls in love with one of his tenants, and as a result, he becomes an advocate for housing reform against the wishes of his family. DVD (Alpha Home Entertainment).

On the Waterfront (1954). Directed by Elia Kazan. An outsider longshoreman finds himself up against violent and corrupt New York harbor unions. DVD (Criterion).

Our Daily Bread (1934). Directed by King Vidor. At the height of the Great Depression, unemployed workers form a commune and set up a socialist farming experiment. DVD (Kanopy); streaming.

The Passaic Textile Strike (1926). Directed by Samuel Russak. Docudrama of the famous New Jersey strike, told from the point of view of the workers. DVD (Image Entertainment).

The Power and the Glory (1933). Directed by William K. Howard. A predecessor of *Citizen Kane*, the film recounts through flashback the rise of a lowly railroad employee to become a ruthless industrialist. DVD (20th Century Fox Home Entertainment).

Quiz Show. (1994). Directed by Robert Redford. Based on a true story, ethnic and class differences between two male contestants fracture amid an ongoing scandal over fixed TV quiz shows. DVD (Walt Disney Studios Home Entertainment); streaming.

Salt of the Earth (1954). Directed by Herbert Biberman. Mexican American women help mobilize a general strike at an exploitative New Mexico zinc mine. DVD (Hoopla Digital); streaming.

Sullivan's Travels (1941). Directed by Preston Sturges. More of a satire of social problem films than a social problem film itself, a self-important Hollywood director pretends to be a hobo as part of his research for the serious film he plans to make. DVD (Universal Studios Home Entertainment).

The Valley of Decision (1945). Directed by Tay Garnett. An Irish maid and the son of a steel mill industrialist fall in love amid a bitter labor strike in 1870s Philadelphia. DVD (Warner Home Video).

Who Pays? (1915). Directed by Harry Harvey, H. M. Horkheimer, and Henry King. The last installment of the 12-part series *Toil and Tyranny* features the tragic consequences of a violent labor strike at a lumber mill that involves a wealthy lumber mill owner, his spoiled daughter, and hotheaded laborers protesting their brutal working conditions. DVD (Image Entertainment).

Wild Boys of the Road (1933). Directed by William Wellman. Two teenage boys run away from home to find work and to help their parents' dire financial circumstances. DVD (Warner Home Video); streaming.

Working Girls (1986). Directed by Lizzie Borden. A day in the life of a brothel, where sex work is about as banal as either housework or the office. DVD (Kanopy); streaming.

RACIAL AND ETHNIC PREJUDICE

American History X (1998). Directed by Tony Kaye. After spending three years in prison for the manslaughter of two black men, a neo-Nazi changes his ways. DVD (New Line Cinema).

Alambrista! (1977). Directed by Robert M. Young. A young Mexican seeks work across the border to provide for his family but faces deportation if caught. DVD (Criterion).

Bad Day at Black Rock (1954). Directed by John Sturges. No one wants to talk to the mysterious one-armed stranger about the hate crime that occurred in a small desert town years ago. Blu-ray (Warner Home Video).

Billy Jack (1971). Directed by T. C. Frank [Tom Laughlin]. Native American ex-Green Beret defends both wild horses and an alternative school from reactionary forces, using karate to bring a message of peace. DVD (Image Entertainment).

Black Legion (1936). Directed by Archie L. Mayo. After being passed over for promotion, a machinist joins a secretive hate group. DVD (Warner Home Video).

The Boy with Green Hair (1948). Directed by Joseph Losey. Allegory of a war orphan and what happens when his hair mysteriously changes color. DVD (Warner Home Video).

Crash (2004). Directed by Paul Haggis. Ethnic and racial tensions intersect and collide amid daily life in Los Angeles. DVD (Lions Gate Entertainment).

Crossfire (1946). Directed by Edward Dmytryk. Just out of the army, a violent psychopath eludes capture from military police investigating the murder of a Jewish man. DVD (Warner Home Video).

The Defiant Ones 1958). Directed by Stanley Kramer. Two escaped convicts must learn to overcome their interracial conflict as they flee from capture. DVD (MGM Home Entertainment); streaming.

Do the Right Thing (1989). Directed by Spike Lee. Ethnic and racial conflicts simmer on a hot summer day in New York's Bedford-Stuyvesant neighborhood. DVD (Criterion).

El Norte (1983). Directed by Gregory Nava. A brother and sister escape harsh conditions in Guatemala and head north to the United States, hoping to find a better life. DVD (Criterion).

The Exiles (1961). Directed by Kent Mackenzie. Native Americans in Los Angeles turn to alcohol to get through Friday night and Saturday morning. DVD (Oscilloscope).

Fury (1936). Directed by Fritz Lang. Narrowly escaping a lynching, an innocent man plots to frame the mob that tried to murder him. DVD (Warner Home Video).

Gentleman's Agreement (1947). Directed by Elia Kazan. A WASP newspaper reporter goes undercover as a Jew to expose polite anti-Semitism in the United States. DVD, Blu-ray (20th Century Fox Home Entertainment).

Guess Who's Coming to Dinner (1967). Directed by Stanley Kramer. A daughter introduces her African American fiancé to her somewhat less open-minded white parents. DVD (Sony Pictures Home Entertainment).

Higher Learning (1995). Directed by John Singleton. A black athlete struggles to come to terms with race, rape culture, and skinheads at a large university campus. DVD (Columbia Pictures).

Home of the Brave (1949). Directed by Mark Robson. Racial tensions boil over during a reconnaissance mission on a remote Japanese island during World War II. DVD (Olive Films).

The House I Live In (1945). Directed by Mervyn LeRoy. Playing himself, Frank Sinatra intervenes in the midst of a gang bullying a boy, with singing and some lessons in religious tolerance. DVD (Hoopla Digital); streaming.

House of Sand and Fog (2003). Directed by Vadim Perelman. An ex-Iranian military officer purchases the house of a woman wrongfully evicted, setting off a sequence of tragic events. DVD (Universal Studios Home Video).

Hungry Hearts (1922). Directed by E. Mason Hopper. Immigrant Russian Jews struggle to survive in New York's Lower East Side. DVD (National Center for Jewish Film).

In the Heat of the Night (1967). Directed by Norman Jewison. An uneasy alliance between a black Detroit detective and a white redneck sheriff forms as the two investigate a murder in the Deep South. DVD, Blu-ray (MGM Home Entertainment).

Intruder in the Dust (1949). Directed by Clarence Brown. Two teenagers and an elderly woman work to save a wrongfully accused black man from a Mississippi lynch mob. DVD (Warner Home Video).

The Lawless (1950). Directed by Joseph Losey. A newspaper editor comes to the defense of Mexican American fruit pickers and soon learns of his town's entrenched racism. DVD (Olive Films).

Lost Boundaries (1949). Directed by Alfred L. Werker. An African American doctor decides to pass for white in order to apply for a hospital position in New Hampshire, only to encounter racism in the military during World War II. DVD (Warner Home Video).

Mixed Blood (1984). Directed by Paul Morrissey. Racism, police corruption, and gang violence all play out amid a Brazilian-Latino drug war on the streets of Manhattan. DVD (Image Entertainment).

Murder in Harlem (1935). Directed by Oscar Micheaux. A woman and a lawyer team up to prove the innocence of her brother, a black night watchman who is framed for murder. DVD (Westlake Entertainment).

Native Land (1942). Directed by Leo Hurwitz and Paul Strand. Wartime docudrama mixing reenactments with actuality to show American freedoms violently under attack. DVD (Flicker Alley).

Nothing but a Man (1964). Directed by Michael Roemer. A proud railroad worker and a schoolteacher encounter racial discrimination in the 1960s Deep South. DVD (New Video).

No Way Out (1950). Directed by Joseph L. Mankiewicz. A bigoted gangster foments race riots after his brother dies in the care of an African American physician. DVD (20th Century Fox Home Entertainment).

Odds against Tomorrow (1959). Directed by Robert Wise. An ex-cop hires a racist ex-con and a black jazz musician with a gambling addiction to rob a small-town bank in upstate New York. What could possibly go wrong? DVD (MGM/UA Home Video).

One Potato, Two Potato (1964). Directed by Larry Peerce. A remarried white woman and her African American spouse fight for custody of their child after the woman's ex-husband takes the battle to court. DVD (Jubilee).

The Pawnbroker (1965). Directed by Sidney Lumet. An emotionally scarred Holocaust survivor struggles to repress his memories while doing business with petty criminals in present-day Harlem. DVD (Olive Films).

Pinky (1949). Directed by Elia Kazan. An African American woman returns to her hometown, passing for white and falling in love with a doctor. DVD (20th Century Fox Home Entertainment).

A Raisin in the Sun (1961). Directed by Daniel Petrie. Living in a cramped Chicago apartment, the matriarch of the Younger family receives the proceeds from a substantial life insurance policy following the death of her husband, exposing long-simmering internal family conflicts and pressures from external societal racism. DVD (Columbia TriStar Home Video).

Skins (2002). Directed by Chris Eyre. The lives of two impoverished Oglala Sioux brothers take very different turns, but the bond between them remains. DVD (Millennium Entertainment); streaming.

Spinning into Butter (2007). Directed by Mark Brokaw. A dean at a university finds herself in the middle of a controversy involving a hate crime. DVD (Screen Media Films).

Street Scene (1930). Directed by King Vidor. Ethnic and domestic conflicts boil over on a hot summer night in an urban slum. DVD (Films Media Group); streaming.

They Won't Forget (1937). Directed by Mervyn LeRoy. In the Deep South, various forces converge to exploit a case involving a pretty female student and her male teacher, wrongfully framed for the girl's murder. DVD (Warner Home Video).

To Sir, with Love (1967). Directed by James Clavell. An idealistic African American teacher takes a post at a mostly white, working-class school in London and comes face-to-face with various shades of racism among both his beleaguered colleagues and the rambunctious students in his class. DVD (Columbia Pictures); streaming.

Trial (1955). Directed by Mark Robson. Both pro- and anti-Communist forces attempt to exploit the case of a Mexican boy framed for the murder of a white girl. DVD (20th Century Fox Home Entertainment). DVD (Warner Home Video).

12 Angry Men (1957). Directed by Sidney Lumet. One man must convince eleven other jurors' certitude, tinged by hasty judgments and prejudice, that there is reasonable doubt a young boy should be convicted for murder and sent to the electric chair.

Within Our Gates (1921). Directed by Oscar Micheaux. The future of an all-black school depends upon an educated but mysterious woman who dedicates her life to saving the institution from the brink of bankruptcy. DVD (Kino Classics).

WOMEN, SEX, AND FAMILY CONFLICT

American Beauty (1999). Directed by Sam Mendes. Trapped within a seemingly perfect but meaningless suburban existence, family members each try to find meaning outside the confines of their home. DVD (Paramount Pictures Home Entertainment).

Blonde Venus (1932). Directed by Josef von Sternberg. When not wearing a gorilla suit, a cabaret singer pursues an adulterous relationship with a millionaire to help pay for her gravely ill husband's cure. DVD (Universal Studios Home Entertainment).

The Easiest Way (1931). Directed by Jack Conway. A woman escapes her dirt-poor background by becoming involved in an extramarital affair with an advertising executive. Then she falls for a reporter. DVD (Warner Home Video).

Fatal Attraction (1987). Directed by Adrian Lyne. A seriously deranged but sexy single woman stalks a happily married man and his family after an extramarital one-night stand. DVD (Paramount Home Entertainment).

North Country (2005). Directed by Niki Caro. Based on one of the first successful sexual harassment suits, a single mother takes a job in a Minnesota mine and takes on a hostile work environment. DVD (Warner Bros. Home Video); streaming.

Sex, Lies, and Videotape (1989). Directed by Steven Soderbergh. An old friend with a video camera comes to stay with a lawyer who is having an affair with his wife's sister. Then the friend videotapes his interviews with the women. DVD (Columbia TriStar Home Video).

Silkwood (1983). Directed by Mike Nichols. Just because you work at a negligent nuclear parts facility in Oklahoma doesn't mean they're not out to get you. DVD (Kino Lorber).

Thelma and Louise (1991). Directed by Ridley Scott. Two women taking a short trip end up fugitives, driving cross-country in a 1966 Thunderbird convertible to elude capture from the police. DVD (MGM Home Video); streaming.

Traffic in Souls (1913). Directed by George Loane Tucker. Working with a cop who also happens to be her boyfriend, a woman tries to save her sister from a prostitution ring and expose the wealthy man running it. DVD (Alpha Video); streaming.

SCREENING PRIVATE ILLNESS AND PUBLIC HEALTH

The Best Years of Our Lives (1946). Directed by William Wyler. Recent veterans of World War II try to adjust to life back in the United States. DVD, Blu-ray (Warner Home Video).

Born on the Fourth of July (1989). Directed by Oliver Stone. A paralyzed Vietnam veteran returns home to become an antiwar activist. DVD, Blu-ray (Universal Studios Home Entertainment).

Coming Home (1978). Directed by Hal Ashby. A woman falls in love with a paraplegic Vietnam veteran while her husband is overseas fighting in the same war. DVD (Kino Lorber).

Days of Wine and Roses (1962). Directed by Blake Edwards. A public relations account executive drags his wife into a downward spiral of alcohol addiction. DVD (Warner Home Video).

A Drunkard's Reformation (1909). Directed by D. W. Griffith. After taking his daughter to see a stage adaptation of Émile Zola's novel *L'Assommoir*, a father recognizes uncanny parallels in his own behavior and decides to change his ways. DVD (Classic Video Streams).

In the Grip of Alcohol (1912). Directed by Gérard Bourgeois. What happens in eight years when you have a sick daughter and an alcohol addiction. No known distributor.

In the Valley of Elah (2007). Directed by Paul Haggis. A retired army investigator works with a young police detective to discover the truth behind his son going AWOL. DVD (Warner Home Video).

The Lost Weekend (1945). Directed by Billy Wilder. A struggling novelist goes on a nightmarish four-day bender in his New York City apartment when he conspires to send both his girlfriend and his brother away to the country for the weekend. DVD (Universal Pictures); streaming.

One Flew Over the Cuckoo's Nest (1975). Directed by Miloš Forman. A likeable misfit feigns insanity so that he can avoid prison. Once inside the mental institution, he organizes the resistance against the asylum's authoritarian regime. DVD (Warner Home Video).

Philadelphia (1993). Directed by Jonathan Demme. A homophobic African American lawyer takes on a lawsuit involving a white lawyer fired by his firm because he has contracted AIDS. DVD (Sony Pictures Home Entertainment); streaming.

Smash Up: The Story of a Woman (1947). Directed by Stuart Heisler. A former nightclub singer sinks deeper into alcoholism and despair after she leaves her career to marry a fellow singer about to break through on the radio. DVD (The Film Detective); streaming.

The Snake Pit (1948). Directed by Anatole Litvak. A woman struggles both with her own repressed memories and the regimentation of a state mental institution. DVD (20th Century Fox Home Entertainment).

The Victims of Alcohol (1902). Directed by Ferdinand Zecca. Yet another early film adaptation of Zola's *L'Assommoir* showing the downward spiral of a family consumed by alcohol. DVD (Oxygéneé).

The Weaker Mind (1913). Directed by Romaine Fielding. Saved from the clutches of a temptress, an engineer reforms his ways and later has the opportunity to save the woman who first plied him with alcohol. No known distributor.

What Drink Did (1909). Directed by D. W. Griffith. A hard worker and devoted family man spirals completely out of control after his colleagues at the wood shop ply him with a few too many drinks. DVD (Classic Video Streams).

When a Man Loves a Woman (1994). Directed by Luis Mandoki. When a wife and mother of two overcomes her alcohol addiction, her controlling husband must face up to his own role as an enabler. DVD (Buena Vista Home Entertainment).

CRIME

Angels with Dirty Faces (1938). Directed by Michael Curtiz. A priest attempts to intervene on the hold his childhood pal, now a hardened criminal, has upon a group of boys. DVD (Warner Bros. Home Video).

Boyz n the Hood (1991). Directed by John Singleton. Three young friends struggle to survive amid a cycle of racism and violence in South Central Los Angeles. DVD, Blu-ray (Sony Pictures Home Entertainment).

Dead End (1935). Directed by William Wyler. The lives of a struggling architect, labor activist, and hardened criminal all converge on a hot summer day in the crucible of a New York slum. DVD (Warner Home Video).

Death Wish (1974). Directed by Michael Winner. When a brutal rape results in the death of his wife, a mild-mannered liberal turns to vigilantism to mete out justice. DVD (Warner Home Video).

Little Caesar (1931). Directed by Mervyn LeRoy. A small-time crook will stop at nothing to get to the top of the crime underworld. DVD (Warner Bros. Home Video); streaming.

Menace II Society (1993). Directed by Albert Hughes and Allen Hughes. A teenager finds himself sinking deeper into the violent quagmire of life in the Watts district of Los Angeles. DVD (Warner Home Video).

The Public Enemy (1931). Directed by William A. Wellman. A small-time hood rises to the top of the Chicago crime syndicate amid Prohibition and gang warfare. DVD, Blu-ray (Warner Home Video); streaming.

Regeneration (1915). Directed by Raoul Walsh. An Irish criminal falls in love with a settlement worker dedicated to improving the welfare of those living under the control of gangsters in New York's Bowery district. DVD (Image Entertainment); streaming.

Traffic (2000). Directed by Steven Soderbergh. Various lives on the US-Mexico border intersect as America escalates its war on drugs and the drug trade. DVD (Universal Studios Home Entertainment); streaming.

OTHER

Jaws (1975). Directed by Steven Spielberg. A great white shark shows up on a New England beach at the height of summer, and he's not looking to perform at Sea World. DVD (Universal Studios Home Entertainment).

Sahara (1943). Directed by Zoltan Korda. Rescued international Allied troops, separated from their units and stranded in the middle of the desert, must work together to face down an impending Nazi attack. DVD (Sony Pictures Home Entertainment).

Index

Addams, Jane, 44, 46, 102
address, mode of, xi, 17, 44, 60, 63, 78, 83, 86
"The Age of Fracture" (Daniel T. Rogers), 12
Alambrista! (1977), 107
American Beauty (1999), 51, 101, 109
American Dream, 6–7, 9, 84, 101
Angels with Dirty Faces (1938), 111
anti-communism, 34–35
American History X (1998), 66, 107

"backlash" against feminism (Susan Faludi), 12, 48, 51, 73
Bad Day at Black Rock (1955), 65, 107
Baer, Robert, 91–92
The Best Year of Our Lives (1946), 16, 77–80, 100, 110
Bernstein, Matthew, 20
Billy Jack (1971), 107
biopics, 105
The Birth of a Nation (1915), 62
Black Fury (1936), 105
Black Legion (1936), 63, 107
blacklisting. *See* Hollywood blacklist
blaxpoitation, 65
Blonde Venus (1932), 45, 109
Blue Collar (1978), 105
Bound for Glory (1978), 105
Boxcar Bertha (1972), 105
The Boy with Green Hair (1948), 107

Boyz n the Hood (1991), 66, 90–91, 111
Brando, Marlon, 34, 88
Brownlow, Kevin, x, xi, 3
Bugsy Malone (1976), 83

Cagle, Chris, x, 9, 19, 25, 72–73
Capital Versus Labor (1910), 5, 105
Cass Timberlane (1947), 105
Central Intelligence Agency (CIA), 92
Chaplin, Charlie, 30
Chicano/a representations, 58–59, 60
child labor, 26–27, 29, 105
Children of Eve (1915), 105
Children Who Labor (1912), 26–27, 29, 105
"cinema of attractions" (Tom Gunning), 5
Clarens, Carlos, 86
Clooney, George, 92
Communist Party, 29
Coursen-Neff, Zama, 26
Cradle Will Rock (1999), 105
Crash (2004), 12, 66, 101, 107
The Crime of Negligence (1912), 105
Crossfire (1946), 8, 63–64, 100, 107
The Cry of the Children (1912), 26, 29, 105

Days of Wine and Roses (1962), 72, 110
Dead End (1937), 20, 111
The Deer Hunter (1978), 106
Dean, James, 88
Death Wish (1974), 111

Index

The Defiant Ones (1958), 20, 64, 107
didacticism, xi, 18, 44, 49–50, 71
"disjunction" in social problem film, 32–33, 34
Do the Right Thing (1989), 12, 66, 90, 108
drug addiction, 106
A Drunkard's Reformation (1909), 70–71, 72, 100, 110

The Easiest Way (1931), 45, 109
Edge of the City (1957), 106
El Norte (1983), 66, 108
Emperor of the North (1973), 106
Empire Zinc Company strike, 33
The Exiles (1961), 66, 108

Fair Labor Standards Act (FLSA), 26
"fallen woman" films, 7, 42, 45, 46
Fatal Attraction (1987), 12, 51, 109
Field, Sally, 36–37
F.I.S.T. (1978), 106
"the forgotten man", 31
"formula" for social problem films, 32
42nd Street (1933), 31
Frank, Leo, 63
Fury (1936), 63, 108

Gaghan, Stephen, 91, 92
gangster films, 83, 84, 86
genre, 3, 4, 12, 15–16. *See also* social problem film
genre hybrids, 31, 63, 83
Gentleman's Agreement (1947), 8, 63–64, 74, 100, 108
Give Us This Day (1949), 106
The Godfather (1972), 84
Gold Diggers of 1933 (1933), 31, 106
The Grapes of Wrath (1940), 7, 17–18, 32, 33, 106
Guess Who's Coming to Dinner (1967), 10, 65, 101, 108
Guthrie, Woody, 105
Griffith, D. W., 62, 70–71, 72, 110, 111

Halliday, George, 90
Heroes for Sale (1933), 106
Higher Learning (1995), 108
Hine, Lewis, 26
Hollywood blacklist, 8, 33, 34, 37, 79

Hollywood film industry, ix, x, 4, 6, 7, 8, 10, 11, 12, 16, 43, 60, 62, 65, 76; censorship/self-regulation, 4, 6, 7–8, 8, 20, 43, 44, 45, 65, 87
Home of the Brave (1949), 19, 100, 108
Hopper, Hedda, 36
The House I Live In (1945), 108
House of Sand and Fog (2003), 66, 108
House Un-American Activities Committee (HUAC), 34, 35, 36
Hughes-Warrington, Marnie, 20
Human Rights Watch, 26
Hungry Hearts (1922), 6, 100, 108

I Am a Fugitive from a Chain Gang (1932), 86
I Can Get It for You Wholesale (1951), 106
I Married a Communist (1949), 106
The Insider (1999), 106
intertextuality, 37
In the Grip of Alcohol (1912), 5, 110
In the Heat of the Night (1967), 108
Iraq War film, 79–80, 110

Jaws (1975), 111
Jenson, Lois, 51, 53
juvenile delinquency, 88, 89

Kazan, Elia, 35, 36
King, Rodney, 90
Klein, Amanda Ann, 17, 20
Kramer, Stanley, 9, 10–11, 107, 108
Ku Klux Klan, 62
Kuhle Wampe or Who Owns the World (1932), 106

"labor-capital films" (Steven J. Ross), 5
labor unions, 105, 106
The Lawless (1950), 108
Little Caesar (1930), 86, 111
Lost Boundaries (1949), 108
The Lost Weekend (1945), 9, 71–72, 72–73, 73, 74, 100, 110
lynching, 62, 63, 108

made-for-television movies, 65
Make Way for Tomorrow (1937), 106
Matewan (1987), 106

melodrama, 5, 17, 41, 77, 86; temperance, 70–71
Menace II Society (1993), 66, 111
Metropolis (1927), 106
Micheaux, Oscar, 61–62, 62–63
Mittell, Jason, 20
Mixed Blood (1984), 108
Modern Times (1936), 30, 31, 106
Murder in Harlem (1935), 63, 108
musicals, 31

narrative, 5, 12, 19–20
National Child Labor Committee (NCLC), 26, 27
Native Land (1942), 108
Navasky, Victor, 35, 36
Neale, Steve, x, 4, 20, 32–33, 77
neo-Nazis, 107
newspapers, 37–38
The New York Times, 37–38
Noriega, Chon, 58–59, 60
Norma Rae (1979), 36–38, 106
North Country (2005), 38, 51–52, 53, 110
Nothing But a Man (1964), 108
No Way Out (1950), 64, 108

Odds Against Tomorrow (1959), 109
One Flew Over the Cuckoo's Nest (1975), 74, 75–77, 110
One Potato, Two Potato (1964), 109
One Third of a Nation (1939), 106
On the Waterfront (1954), 34, 35, 36, 39, 106
Our Daily Bread (1934), 106

The Passaic Textile Strike (1926), 29, 107
The Pawnbroker (1965), 65, 109
Philadelphia (1993), 77–79, 80, 110
Pinky (1949), 18, 109
Poitier, Sidney, 64
political ideology, x–xi, 8, 9, 10–11, 11, 12, 19, 37, 48, 49–50, 51, 60, 79
The Power and the Glory (1933), 107
psychology/psychiatry, 64, 71, 74, 77
The Public Enemy (1931), 17, 86, 111

Quiz Show (1994), 107

Raisin in the Sun (1961), 62, 109

realism, xi, 9, 12, 20
Rebel Without a Cause (1955), 88
reception, audience and critical, ix, x, xi, 4, 20, 37, 52
Reds (1982), 30
Reed, John, 30
Regeneration (1915), 111
Ritt, Martin, 37
Rockefeller, John D., Jr., 43
Rogin, Michael, 31
Rosen, Ruth, 45
Rosenstone, Robert A., 53
Ross, Steven J., 29. *See also* "labor-capital films"

Sahara (1943), 111
Salt of the Earth (1954), 33, 34, 39, 57, 58–59, 107
Scarface (1932), 86
Scarface (1984), 84
"search for order" (Robert Wiebe), 4
Silkwood (1983), 48–50, 53, 110
Silkwood, Karen, 48–55, 52, 53
Singleton, John, 90, 91
Skins (2002), 66, 109
Sloan, Kay, x, 5, 18, 43, 70, 71
The Smash-Up (1947), 72, 110
The Snake Pit (1948), 74–75, 76–77, 110
social reform, x, 3, 4, 6, 7, 8, 19, 41, 42, 44–45, 48, 70, 74–75, 77
sociology, 3, 19
The Sopranos (1999–2007), 88
Spinning Into Butter (2007), 109
Stamp, Shelley, 46
star text, 88–89
Stone, Oliver, 91
Street Scene (1930), 109
subgenres, 83
Sullivan's Travels (1941), 107
Supreme Court decisions, 6, 7, 8, 10, 44
Sutton, Crystal Lee, 36, 38
Sweet Sweetback's Baadasssss Song (1971), 65
Syriana (2005), 91–92

Taft-Hartley Act, 33
television, 65
Thelma and Louise (1991), 12, 51, 110
They Won't Forget (1937), 63, 109

To Sir, With Love (1967), 109
Traffic (2000), 12, 91, 111
Traffic in Souls (1913), 42–45, 46–48, 100, 110
Trial (1955), 65, 109
12 Angry Men (1957), 65, 109

The Valley of Decision (1945), 107
The Victims of Alcohol (1901)
Vietnam War films, 9, 11, 79–80, 101, 106, 110

Wall Street (1987), 90, 91
Warner Bros., 63
Warshow, Robert, 88
The Weaker Mind (1913), 71, 72, 111

When a Man Loves a Woman (1994), 71, 72, 73, 111
What Drink Did (1909), 70, 72, 100, 111
Who Pays? (1915), 107
whistleblowers, 106
Wild Boys of the Road, 107
The Wild One (1953)
Within Our Gates (1920), 62, 109
The Woman on Pier 13. See *I Married a Communist* (1949)
Working Girls (1986), 107

X rating, 65

Zanuck, Darryl F., 74

About the Authors

Jennifer Frost teaches and researches Hollywood, film, and 20th-century US domestic politics and social history at the University of Auckland, New Zealand. She has taught the course Hollywood's America: 20th Century U.S. History through Hollywood Film for over a decade, has contributed to the scholarship of teaching and learning history, and brings those experiences to this book. Her books include *Hedda Hopper's Hollywood: Celebrity Gossip and American Conservatism* (2011) and *Producer of Controversy: Stanley Kramer, Hollywood Liberalism, and the Cold War* (2017).

Steven Alan Carr is professor and chair of communication and directs the Institute for Holocaust and Genocide Studies at Purdue University Fort Wayne. He also served as a fellow in residence at the US Holocaust Memorial Museum Center for Advanced Holocaust Study in 2002–2003. Carr has written many essays on film history, especially addressing Hollywood during the 1930s and 1940s, and his current project explores the American film industry's response to Nazi anti-Semitism and, eventually, the Holocaust. He is the author of *Hollywood and Anti-Semitism: A Cultural History Up to World War II* (2001).

www.ingramcontent.com/pod-product-compliance
Lightning Source LLC
Chambersburg PA
CBHW032048300426
44117CB00009B/1238